the Musician's Walk

An Ethical Labyrinth

G-6734

the Musician's Walk

An Ethical Labyrinth

The third in a trilogy with

The Musician's Soul

and

The Musician's Spirit

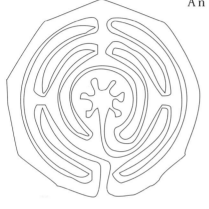

James Jordan

Photography by
Eric Kephart

Foreword by

Weston Noble

With essays by

James Abbington

Richard Floyd

Allegra Martin

L. Jackson Newell

Kenneth R. Raessler

John Yarrington

GIA Publications, Inc.
Chicago

Photo by Br. Emmanuel Morinelli, O.C.S.O.

The Musician's Walk: An Ethical Labyrinth
James Jordan

Photographs by Eric Kephart. Used with permission.
Photographs by Br. Emmanuel Morinelli, O.C.S.O. Used with permission.
Dust Jacket Photograph by Dan Niven. Used with permission.
Illustrations and Layout by Martha Chlipala.

G-6734
ISBN: 1-57999-550-0
Copyright © 2006 GIA Publications, Inc.
7404 S. Mason Avenue, Chicago, IL 60638

Dedication

This book cannot be dedicated to one person, but rather several who have been part of my Walk. The book is large, and The Walk has been long.

To Elizabeth Jordan
She is my life's inspiration.

My daughter has taught me more about living than she will ever know. This book is dedicated to her, all juvenile diabetics, and all who cope daily with chronic conditions who walk their walk with courage, hope, and a deep appreciation of life and its beauty. May the future of stem cell research hold a cure.

And others who have taught me things about The Walk.

Leslie Jordan
Lori Jordan
Donald Stoppi
John Brennan
Bernard Kunkel
Donna Ippoliti
Eric Kephart
Dean Roger Dougherty
George Miller
Mark Kelleher
William Payn
Kay Payn
Daniel Payn
Marilyn Shenenberger
William Hammer
Janet Yamron
Rae Jean Teeter
Marc Persing
Margaret Persing
Rita Richard
Christopher Ross
Donald Beckie
John Scott
Blanaid Murphy
Frederick Jarrett
Catherine Jarrett
Roger Ames
Eileen Hollen
Phillip Green
Gail B. Poch
Veronica Kryscio
John Kryscio
Charles B. Adukaitis

A portion of the profits of this book will be given to the American Diabetes Association. www.diabetes.org

"Wakefulness is the way to life."

"From His Point of View"

Table of Contents

section one: on the threshold

section three: the resting place

section four: journeying out

"Music is the home of the spirit!"

"Cradled Sphere"

Foreword

by

Weston Noble

Robert Shaw once said, "Music is the voice of the spirit." After searching for the depth of meaning inherent in these special words, I have come to rephrase it slightly to read, "Music is the home of the spirit!" Recently, I discovered James Jordan's *The Musician's Soul.* My journey of discovery continues.

A musician without the understanding of the spiritual life within is missing the font of inspiration. To verbalize such a necessity is a unique challenge. How grateful we are to Dr. Jordan for his *Musician's Walk* in crystallizing an area that all but defies definition!

"...each in their own way has contributed a valuable aspect..."

"The Last One Standing"

Acknowledgments

I foolishly thought many years ago that books were the effort of one person. Of the many gifts I have received from writing, the one I value most is my newly acquired "awe" of the collaborative will of many. I am humbled and deeply gratified that so many people agreed willingly and enthusiastically to be part of this book. Each in their own way has contributed a valuable aspect of what you will read, whether through the written word or through artistic creativity. I realized early on that while this subject matter was important, I needed people who I respected and admired to help me create a higher level of awareness by sharing their experiences.

My thanks to James Abbington, Richard Floyd, Allegra Martin, L. Jackson Newell, Kenneth R. Raessler, and John Yarrington. Their viewpoints have deeply enriched this volume, and all have influenced my thought along the way. Some are long-time friends who have been in my life for many years, and some are newfound spirits who walked across my own path. I feel in a very strange way that Jimmie, Dick, Allegra, Jack, Ken, and John are now walking the same path because of this collaboration. Also, special thanks to Brother Emmanuel Morinelli for his wonderful photographs, taken at the Trappist Abbey in Spencer, Massachusetts. And thanks to Richard Mayne for bringing the work of Hawkins to my attention.

The creative "team" at GIA who has taken on this book and its message as if it were their own can never be thanked enough. Martha Chlipala has created a visual design for this book that serves both as an illustrative work of art and a source of inspiration as one makes his or her way through these pages. Her gifts as an illustrator and designer will be obvious to all who view this book. It was her artistic vision that gave my words a vibrant visual life. The design of this book provides visual respites as one makes his or her way through the "walk" of this book.

To my editor, Linda Vickers. Good editors are hard to find. Great editors are a rarity, and Linda is exactly that. With great care, Linda has taken this very personal content and massaged it into shape as if it were her own. Aside from being my editor, she has become my friend. Without her, this book would never have been what it has become.

My life has been blessed by the presence of one Eric Kephart. Being around such a creative being teaches one much about being an artist in this world. As a multi-faceted visual and performing artist, I have marveled and learned through his eyes how to see the world in a more luminous and vibrant way. His gifted eye on the world through his photography graces this entire book. You will see several photos labeled "totem." These are path markers that appear on the many hiking trails in Sedona, Arizona. Just as those totems have marked the correct path for hikers in Arizona, Eric's very presence has been a path totem in my life. To say "Thanks" is simply insufficient to express my deepest gratitude for what he has contributed to this book and to my life.

Thanks to Alec Harris and Edward Harris at GIA. Books such as this can only be created when one is given a certain freedom to think "outside of the box." Their deep commitment to the education of musicians and to my work can never be repaid. Few authors have enjoyed such support and encouragement. Their vision and support of all the authors now associated with GIA has created a great resource for musicians and music educators.

And thanks to Sedona, Arizona. With the exception of the photographs taken at the Abbey in Spencer, all of the photographs in this book were taken in Sedona, Arizona. For those who have visited that place, I need not provide any further explanation of its beauty and rejuvenative power. For those musicians and artists who have never visited, I encourage you to do it. My annual trips there provide

xviii

me refreshed perspective and deep insight about the world and my life. A majority of the words in this book were either written in Sedona or conceived as a result of my time in Sedona. What was not written in Sedona was written in the beautiful Starbucks on Lake Afton in Yardley, Pennsylvania!

Rider University has generously provided two research leaves that gave me the "space" to write this book. The sabbatical in 2003 allowed me to complete the manuscript, and the sabbatical during the 2005–06 academic year allowed me time to complete the production end of this project. I am deeply appreciative of their generous support of my work.

And finally, thanks to Edwin Gordon. Dr. Gordon, through example, taught me about language, thinking, and the creative life through the written word. As I read the words I write, I can only be deeply appreciative of his ability to impart by both example and word. My "walk" with him has made all the difference.

And for that, I am deeply grateful.

James Jordan

Yardley, Pennsylvania

"...what it is that inspires the artist..."

"Solitary View"

*About the Photography
and Design of This Book*

p h o t o g r a p h y

The photographs included in this book represent two different years
of time (2004 and 2005) spent in Sedona, Arizona. As an artist, my
trips to Sedona are times of inner-reflection, connection to the earth
and nature, and the universe. These are times for me to reflect upon
the past, to clear away, and to cultivate new plans, goals, and dreams
for the near and distant future.

Anyone who has traveled to Sedona can tell you that it is an
"internalizing" experience. The natural, universal energy that is so
present in Sedona gets to the core of a person immediately upon
arriving. But the experience is so beyond the "personal," which is
what I tried to convey through the photographs that appear in the
book. Many were selected because of their "universal" appeal. These
images—sunsets, landscapes, trees, plants—speak of "our connection" to nature inasmuch as our respectful coexistence with it. Other
images were selected for their "textural" appeal. My intent is to draw
you to the image because you want to touch it, feel it, experience the
sensation, and share it. The "art" photographs were selected for their

"inspirational" appeal. Many were taken during my hikes up Bell Rock, a rock formation that sits on an energy vortex in Sedona. Finally, several images speak of a path—a path we find ourselves on, or even following in life, with or without the realization of why we are on the path. To be committed to a path or life's mission is oftentimes very hard, but it is my time spent in Sedona that reinforces what it is that I do as an artist every day. Most importantly, all of my images represent my fascination with this place of such awesome beauty and inspiration. To musicians and to all who read this book, it is my hope that you will at least have the opportunity to experience what it is for me to travel to such a magical place—and what it is that inspires the artist, the creator, the magician, and the musician in all of us.

Eric Kephart

illustrations and layout

When I was asked to work on *The Musician's Walk*, I was excited, thankful, and a little apprehensive. The previous two books in the trilogy had established a standard and a style that was now my task to duplicate.

After reading the book and discussing it with my co-workers, I envisioned the theme. Reflecting the content of the text, it was to be journalistic with a private, introspective look.

I began by utilizing the same layout that was established in *The Musician's Spirit*, but this time I changed the headings by using a font called P22 Cezanne Regular. This "inky" font gave the title pages a handwritten quality and helped to set the tone for the entire book.

In keeping with the theme, the author, Alec Harris (GIA), and I decided that the illustrations should appear like fine-line ink drawings, as if the author were sketching or doodling in the margins.

Special attention was paid to Eric Kephart's beautiful photos. The goal was to match each photo with the content of the chapter. I also pulled quotes from the chapters and combined them with the photos to give the reader a "visual taste" of each chapter.

Reflecting on labyrinths, I began to draw versions of the more famous examples. I then expanded my scope by including illustrations that reflected the labyrinth theme as well as the content of the surrounding text.

It is my hope that my illustrations visually "season" the text, adding texture or an extra dimension to the content. These drawings can be found throughout the book...I hope you enjoy them.

Martha Chlipala

"Hear, and your soul shall live..." Isaiah 55:3

"Flor"

Introduction

All my life I've struggled to be an honest musician—and now you want me to be a conductor. (p. 340)

Paul Hindemith
The   Robert   Shaw   Reader

Estranged from the music of our own lives, we endure our ordinary days with existential anxiety. We worry about the past and anticipate the future. All the while overlooking the season of the moment. If we were to embrace the past without excessive judgment and calmly step, not leap, into the future, we might feel the vitality of the all-embracing soul.

The principle of being present to life is also complicated by the soul's odd sense of time, so different from the literal measurements of the clock and calendar. The soul exists in cycles of time, full of repetition, and it has equal portions of flowing temporarality and static eternity. Responsive to the soul, we may easily drift out of literal life several times a day to revisit people and places of the past or imagine the

xxvi

future. These visitations are entirely different from the ego's anxious attempts to resolve the past or control the future. They are more like a summer's week on the beach, a way to get away and find a fresh perspective. (p. 7)

Thomas Moore
Original Self

Wakefulness is the way to life.
The fool sleeps as if he were already dead,
But the master is awake and he lives forever.
He watches. He is clear.
How happy he is! For he sees that wakefulness is life.
How happy he is following the path of the awakened.
With great perseverance he meditates, seeking freedom
And happiness.

Gautama the Buddha
Dhammapada

The world is too dangerous for anything but truth and too small for anything but love.
We can never really love anybody with whom we never laugh.
Love is in the giver, not the gift.

William Sloane Coffin

Love is the difficult realization that something other than oneself is real.

> Iris Murdoch
> ───────────

You are just living in a small corner of your being the tiny conscious mind. It is as if somebody has a palace and has completely forgotten about the palace and has started living on the porch and thinks that this is all. (p. 10)

> Osho
> ───────────
> *Awareness*

Some of us get woken up by the harsh realities of life. We suffer so much that we wake up. But people keep bumping again and again into life. They still go on sleepwalking. They never wake up. Tragically, it never occurs to them that there may be another way. It never occurs to them that there may be a better way. Still, if *you* haven't been bumped sufficiently by life, and you haven't suffered enough, then there is another way: to *listen*. I don't mean you have to agree with what I'm saying. That wouldn't be listening. Believe me, it really doesn't matter whether you agree with what I'm saying or you don't. Because agreement and disagreement have to do with words and concepts and theories. They don't have anything to do with truth. Truth is never expressed in words. Truth is sighted suddenly, as a result of a certain attitude. (pp. 16–17)

In awareness you change, but you've got to experience it. At this point you're just taking my word for it. Perhaps also you've got a plan to become aware. Your ego, in its own cunning way, is trying to push you into awareness. Watch it! You'll meet with resistance; there will be trouble. When someone is anxious about being aware all the time, you can spot the mild anxiety. They want to be awake, to find out if they're really awake or not. That's part of *asceticism*, not awareness. (pp. 145–146)

Anthony de Mello

A w a r e n e s s

In every artist's development the germ of the latter work is always found in the earlier. The nucleus around which the artist's intellect builds his work is himself...and this changes little from birth to death.

The only real influence I've ever had was myself. (p. xii)

Edward Hopper

The Soul's Code by James Hillman

Human being is never sheer being; it is always involved in meaning. The dimension of meaning is as indigenous to his being human as the dimension of space is to stars and stones. Just as man occupies a position in space, so has he a status in what may be called metaphorically a dimension of meaning. He is involved even when unaware of it. He may be creative or destructive; he cannot live outside it. The concern for meaning, the gist of all creative efforts, is not self-imposed; it is a necessity of his being. (p. 51)

Abraham Joshua Heschel

W h o   I s   M a n ?

*I*deas and concepts often present themselves like lightning bolts. I was sitting in a lecture on Body Mapping with Barbara Conable. A question came from someone in the class concerning the need to "focus" on a particular body part to achieve efficient and good function. Barbara replied by saying that the worst thing musicians could do is focus or concentrate. What a musician needs to develop is awareness not focus.

While it may be a semantic twist of words, it is an important—even life-changing—change of attitude. As I pondered the concept, its potency for musicians became overwhelmingly apparent. The implications overwhelmed me. Hence, the birth of this book.

I have never understood trilogies. Some writers claim that ideas, in order to be complete, have three core principles that develop in the author's unconscious mind over the span of a life. In *The Musician's Soul* (GIA, 1999), I tried to set out how one begins to explore one's inwardness and spirituality, and how that exploration can open up new worlds of music making. In The *Musician's Spirit* (GIA, 2002), I attempted to convince musicians of the power of their personal life stories and how their stories could help them connect with those with whom they make music. I also wanted to explore the "why" concerning musicians' relationships with those who surround them.

xxx This book can be considered the third of a trilogy of sorts. *The Musician's Walk* will attempt to define what it is to be an aware musician and, consequently, an alive human being. I want to share with you the many ways musicians must be aware and explain why the concept of focus and concentration is detrimental to the music-making process. But more importantly, this book would make more sense if one has explored the issues in *The Musician's Soul* and *The Musician's Spirit.*

Many have said one must "keep the big picture in mind throughout life." That is the course of this book. It is to remind musicians of the many human pitfalls they face each day and to look at their musical journey as part of life, not detached from it. It is also important to real- ize that the journey is not a straight or simple one. It convolutes, turns, and acquires people, care, and love along the way. I have strong feelings that musicians and artists, or at least the ones who struggle so, don't under-  stand their journey let alone themselves. Many hide behind the guise of making music, never realizing that each musical experience and human connection to human beings shapes the path and direction of their journey. Understanding what one's journey has

been and what it will be is the beginning of awareness, which should
permeate all one does.

   As I review in my mind's eye the truly amazing musicians (and
for that matter, the great teachers), they were or are not focused
human beings. They go beyond being alive and in the moment. They
are *aware*—constantly. Their entire music making grows out of that
awareness: a constant awareness of their spiritual self, an awareness
at all times of the sound being created, and an awareness of all the
human beings with whom they are making music. Many
persons have labeled this as "being alive" which, while a noble
concept, is similar to the philosophical ideas of the semantics of the
words "truth" and "beauty." One gains understanding of truth and
beauty by studying its semantic subparts to gain an in-depth understanding. Being alive as a musician is, more directly stated, being
aware—at all times. It is this total awareness that translates the work
of *The Musician's Soul* and *The Musician's Spirit* into a living
presence that illuminates the composer's intent. This awareness needs
to include a kind of philosophical awareness, an inclusive body
kinesthetic awareness and a movement awareness.

   The concept seems so simplistic. I have found that most
life-changing concepts are the result of clarifying language and
semantics so meaning becomes clearer. To become an aware musician
is the final part of the musician's journey. To be fully aware (not

xxxii

focused) is to be totally aware of oneself—devoid of ego—and the world in which one exists. When awareness is brought to music making after some important internal spiritual exploration and life storying, the human energy imparted unlocks the true nature of the art we love and adore.

The end of the journey is as important as its beginning. But awareness of the journey must be at the core of what you do. Soul, spirit through story, and finally an awareness of journey will profoundly deepen all our experiences and teach so much more to our children than just notes and rhythms.

To become conscious of anything we have first to get the words right, because words are loaded with implications. (p. 12)

James Hillman
Kinds of Power

Section One

On the Threshold

"...a single clear path into an interior reality,"

"The Way Right"

Chapter 1

The Musician's Walk: A Labyrinth?

The Labyrinth taught me when you get knocked off your path by others to stay calm and continue, one step at a time. (p. 56)

At the center, I met myself waiting there for me... (p. 56)

Labyrinth Pilgrims

The Healing Labyrinth by Helen Raphael Sands

"Archetypal images," Jung says, "decide the fate of man." Jung placed archetypes at the center of his psychological theory, and brought them to our attention. He defined an archetype as "a figure—be it daimon, a human being, or a process—that constantly recurs in the course of history and appears wherever creative fantasy is freely expressed." These forms exist independent of the human psyche in the collective unconscious and are governed by their own laws. They include figures—spirals, trees—and geometric designs—circles, squares, triangles. The collective unconscious is the invisible realm of symbols and forms that are free floating throughout our world. The forms in

4

the collective unconscious are universal. They can be found in art and religious symbology all over the world. The labyrinth is simply one example of archetype. (p. 150)

The archetype that is enlivened in the labyrinth is the archetype of transformation. The circle, which expresses wholeness and unity, is the central archetype, which Jung called the self. (p. 152)

Lauren Artress
Walking a Sacred Path

To begin with, for many people today, the labyrinth symbolizes a *way in*, a single clear path into an interior reality, a track through the layers of their consciousness, past the confusion and the chaos of the daily world. We should not underestimate the power of this metaphor. A path, like a door, is very seductive; it offers the promise of excitement and new discoveries but also of guidance in times of trouble, a way through the maze of life. (p. 14)

Virginia Westbury
Labyrinths

The labyrinth deepens self-awareness, releases creativity, increases concentration, and quiets the mind. Following the path to the end aids those who need to bring closure to unfinished tasks. Putting one foot in front of the other, with no end in sight, teaches perseverance. Sometimes the path of the labyrinth can mimic experiences in life. (p. 273)

Craig Wright
The Maze and the Warrior

During a labyrinth walk the left and right hemispheres of the brain are balanced, leading to the perfect state for accessing intuition and creativity. We let go of our typical linear and analytical ways of thinking and move into a more creative and intuitive awareness. (p. 11)

The labyrinth's gift is simplicity, both the simplicity of stripping away all external do's and don'ts to listen to our own voices and the simplicity of the walk itself. No advanced degrees are necessary to master the labyrinth, no long training sessions, no technical manuals. (p. 13)

Melissa Gayle West
Exploring the Labyrinth

Is there a guide for the labyrinth of man? The necessity of guidance is a mode of being human. Animal life is a straight path; the inner life is a maze, and no one can find his way through or about without guidance. Such is the condition from which there is no escape.

One thing that sets man apart from animals is a boundless, unpredictable capacity for the development of an inner universe. There is more potentiality in his soul than in any other being known to us. Look at the infant and try to imagine the multitude of events it is going to engender. Indeed, the enigma of the human being is not in what he is but what he is able to be. (p. 39)

Abraham Joshua Heschel
Who Is Man?

6   Yet, a skeptical voice might ask, if balance and relaxation are needed, why not play a game of chess and go for a swim, or do a crossword puzzle and take a walk in the woods? Indeed, what are the special curative properties of the labyrinth? Personal testimony suggests that the healing powers of the labyrinth rest in its peculiar configuration: the all-inclusive circular design encourages a feeling of unity and community; the boundary of the labyrinth sets limits of human behavior, just as do walls of monastic community; the complicated path forces concentration; and the center, reached after much labor, provides the perfect place to "center" one's personality and be closer to God, all within a protected space. (p. 274)

Craig Wright

The   Maze   and   the   Warrior

I have always found paradigms to be extremely helpful when working through problems or gaining new insights and understandings. In a recent visit to a church in Philadelphia, I happened into a labyrinth "walking." I had long forgotten about labyrinths, both their aesthetic magic and their ability to redirect and refocus the human spirit. I first experienced this as an undergraduate when visiting Chartres Cathedral. I remember being given a paper with instructions on how to "walk" the labyrinth in that cathedral. What I remember most about navigating the labyrinth is that it forced me to make directional decisions; but those directional decisions were not unlike decisions I was making in my life at that

The Musician's Walk

time. I vividly remember encountering people who were also walking the labyrinth that day. Some walked; some stopped after a change in direction. But what was most remarkable about the walk through the labyrinth was when I finally arrived at center. As I reached center, I stood there silently with others. We all seemed to be at an incredible peace. It seemed that since we had completed this "maze," our reward was an arrival at center, a place of peace and calm.

When one walks a labyrinth, the journey through its turns can be divided into four distinct movements:

1) On the threshold

2) Journeying in

3) The resting place

4) Journeying out

Each movement adds a new element to your experience: waiting and gathering yourself at the threshold gives way to movement and to realizing who you are at that moment; your journey in opens your mind and lets thoughts and emotions flow freely; your arrival at the center allows you to rest and opens up the possibility of a new awareness being born; your journey out allows you to return with this awareness. (p. 56)

Helen Raphael Sands
The Healing Labyrinth

a short history of labyrinths

Labyrinths were very popular during medieval times. As many as twenty-two of the eighty Gothic cathedrals housed labyrinths. In our present day, we are experiencing a rediscovery of the labyrinth as a spiritual tool. Many communities are coming together to construct labyrinths in their community parks. Spiritual centers are creating them for those on retreat. Hospitals are building permanent labyrinths for patients and staff. Cancer support groups use labyrinths for strength and finding one's way through difficult times. Patients at hypertension clinics walk labyrinths to reduce stress, the staff use them for taking a much-needed time-out during a stress-filled day. But perhaps the age-old labyrinth holds another way for musicians to come to center and calm themselves in a chaotic world.

The eleven-circuit labyrinth is the one most widely replicated today. In the early 1990s, two such labyrinths were created at Grace Cathedral in San Francisco. Hundreds of thousands of visitors have walked these Cathedral labyrinths, and the idea has proliferated from there. As of this writing, hundreds of eleven-circuit labyrinths are being created around the world.

There are also the classical seven-circuit labyrinth and the eleven-circuit medieval labyrinth, both non-linear. Many persons prefer to make these labyrinths in sand. By using sand to trace the labyrinth, an important tactile element is added. Sand is a sensuous, easy-to-move material that will allow one's natural flow to come forth. And the use of natural materials allows an energetic flow between the pattern and the person using it.

the labyrinth: a powerful paradigm for the musician's walk

As an engineer, spiritual person, and recovering Catholic I have to say that walking the Chartres labyrinth has two functions. One, to calm the spirit and the other to balance the brain. If you look at the Cretan labyrinth, it looks like a cross section of the brain. By walking it as well as the Chartrain one, you balance all quadrants, hence institute healing on many levels. (p. 274)

Craig Wright
The Maze and the Warrior

In writing this book, it occurred to me that there is perhaps no better paradigm for the musician's walk than that of the labyrinth. A beautiful design, it is a physical representation of the music we make in the aesthetic sense: balanced, symmetrical, and engaging. But upon closer examination, the labyrinth can be a physical paradigm of the walk of the musician. Ours is a walk toward center; turns and challenges face us every day, especially when

dealing with other musicians. In dealing with others, we experience difficulties when we refuse to change direction "because of the music" or to examine a possible change in course to deepen our music making because our compassion and understanding of others has deepened.

It also occurred to me that many musicians, unfortunately, enter such a life labyrinth with music "strapped to their back" so to speak. When they reach a turning point, they refuse to follow outside influence or their own souls; they plant themselves in one place, perhaps for the rest of their professional lives. It is those musicians who make constant changes of direction when learning to deal with people and life around them, and then move in another direction. All the changes of direction, just like the labyrinth, move them closer to their center and, ultimately, the center and core of the musical experience.

Walking the labyrinth also gives rise to certain strong emotions that are not unlike those musicians face in musical contexts, such as anxiety (Will I be able to find my way?) or impatience (Why is the person in front of me moving so slowly?) or anger (Why do I always have to give way to people on the path?). The labyrinth is both a mirror and a teacher, telling you something very directly about yourself. Above all, you learn not to suppress feelings but to embrace them and move on.

Finally, it occurred to me that if a musician is able to arrive at his/her spiritual core, just like the labyrinth walkers, then a calm, peace, and solitude would allow the musician to let his/her music making be powerful and compelling. The musician's walk *is* a labyrinth—a maze of choices and changes in direction that must be embraced, recognized, and respected as part of the larger journey in a musical life.

Thus, you will find that the content of this book is arranged according to the path through which the labyrinth guides you: 1) on the threshold, (2) journeying in, (3) the resting place, and (4) journeying out. The chapters attempt to describe some of the changes in direction, from understanding how to "be" when with colleagues to learning how to "be" when sound is present. It is a type of awareness that, when fostered and nourished, will raise one's musicianship to new levels of human experience.

I strongly encourage readers of this book to ponder the wonders of the labyrinth. Each of us should "walk the walk" of a real labyrinth. Its portioning of physical space causes one to be aware of self in a new way. Music making is not unlike the walk in a labyrinth. When we walk with others, we are confronted with whether to connect or disconnect. We are confronted with decisions. We may even be asked to sublimate ourselves and move out of the way for another. And when we finally arrive at the center of a labyrinth, a certain centeredness

12

and rootedness overcomes us. The labyrinth is a blueprint for being with others who occupy the same space. Is there any greater paradigm for musicians?

Humans have always believed in the power of symbols, and it is their capacity to do so that separates traditional faith from modern scientific inquiry. Though the warrior and his sparring partner have disappeared from the labyrinth, the symbol endures. As it has for more than four thousand years, the maze today continues to provide enjoyment, comfort, instruction, and nourishment for yet another age. It remains a sign of a timeless human search for guidance in this world and a rational path to the next. (p. 275)

Craig Wright

The Maze and the Warrior

additional labyrinth resources

Artress, Lauren. *Walking a Sacred Path: Rediscovering the Labyrinth as a Spiritual Tool.* New York: Riverhead Books, 1995.

Schafer, Donna. *Labyrinths from the Outside In.* Woodstock, VT: Skylight Paths, 2000.

West, Melissa Gayle. *Exploring the Labyrinth.* New York: Broadway Books, 2000.

Westbury, Virginia. *Labyrinths: Ancient Paths of Wisdom and Peace.* New York: Da Capo Press, 2001.

Wright, Craig. *The Maze and the Warrior: Symbols in Architecture, Theology and Music.* Cambridge, MA: Harvard University Press, 2001.

"When we walk onto the stage, we enter into light..."

"Ritual"

Chapter 2

Moving into Light and Wakefulness

What is the popular conception of the artist? Gather a thousand descriptions, and the resulting composite is the portrait of a moron: he is held to be childish, irresponsible, and ignorant or stupid in everyday affairs.

The picture does not necessarily involve censure or unkindness. These deficiencies are attributed to the intensity of the artist's preoccupation with his particular kind of fantasy and to the unworldly nature of the fantastic itself. The bantering tolerance granted to the absentminded professor is extended to the artist. Biographers contrast the artlessness of his judgments with the high attainment of his art, and while his naiveté or rascality are gossiped about, they are viewed as signs of Simplicity and Inspiration, which are the handmaidens of Art. And if the artist is inarticulate and lacking in the usual repositories of fact and information, how fortunate, it is said, that nature has contrived to divert him from all worldly distractions so he may be single-minded in regards to his special office. (p. 1)

Mark Rothko

The Artist's Reality

16

The purpose of art is not the release of a momentary ejection of adrenaline but is, rather, the gradual, lifelong construction of a state of wonder and serenity.

Glenn Gould, interview

Musical America (1962)

It seems to me that before a man tries to express anything to the world, he must recognize in himself an individual, a new one, very distinct from others. (p. 135)

A work of art is a trace of a magnificent struggle. (p. 271)

Robert Henri

The Art Spirit

The drama of the human condition comes solely from consciousness. Of course, consciousness and its revelations allow us to create a better life for self and others, but the price we pay for better life is high. It is not just the price of risk and danger and pain. It is the price of knowing risk, danger, and pain. Worse even: it is the price of knowing what pleasure is and *knowing* when it is missing or unattainable.

The drama of the human condition thus comes from consciousness because it concerns knowledge obtained in a bargain that none of us struck: the cost of a better existence is the loss of innocence about that very existence. The feeling of what happens is the answer to a question we never asked, and it is also the coin in a Faustian bargain that we could have never negotiated. Nature did it for us. (p. 316)

Antonio Damasio

The Feeling of What Happens

Walk s'naicisuM ehT

For I have learned

To look on nature, not as in the hour
Of thoughtless youth; but hearing oftentimes
The still, sad music of humanity,
Nor harsh nor grating, though of ample power
To chasten and subdue. And I have felt
A presence that disturbs me with the joy
Of elevated thoughts; a sense of sublime
Of something far more deeply interfused,
Whose dwelling is the light of setting suns,
And the round ocean and the living air,
And the blue sky, and in the mind of man;
A motion and a spirit, that impels
All thinking things, all objects of all thought,
And rolls through all things. Therefore am I still
A lover of the meadows and the woods,
And mountains; and of all that we behold
From this green earth; of all the mighty world
Of eye, and ear,—both what they half create,
And what perceive; well pleased to recognise [*sic*]
In nature and the language of the sense,
The anchor of my purest thoughts, the nurse,
The guide, the guardian of my heart, and soul
Of all my moral being.

William Wordsworth

from lines composed
a few miles above
Tintern Abbey

It may be more important to be awake than to be successful, balanced or healthy. What does it mean to be awake? Perhaps to be living with a lively imagination, responding honestly and courageously to opportunity and avoiding the temptation to follow mere habit or collective values. It means to be an individual, in every instance manifesting the originality of who we are. This is the ultimate form of creativity— following the lead of the deep soul as we make a life.

We all fall asleep and allow life to rush by without reflection and consideration. When we are shocked into awareness by tragedy or failure, this is the time not simply to make resolutions for the future, but to choose to live an awakened life. The Buddha was called "the awakened one." (pp. 126–127)

Thomas Moore

The Original Self

*A*s conductors or soloists, most of us have had the experience of walking onto a concert stage. We stand in a darkened area of the stage wing waiting for the appropriate moment, hidden from the musicians, the audience, and the world at large. When we walk onto the stage, we enter into light and into the eyesight of audience and other performers. We move into a situation where the light of the room illuminates the musicians and us.

Walk s'naicisuM ehT

This oft-repeated performance pattern is one that has an unusual correlation with our lives as artists. If we think of those times when we walked onto a stage, there is an unusual awareness that overcomes us. The lights and the human focus in the room cause a heightened sense of awareness of self. This heightened sense of self almost always ensures a better performance than in the practice room or rehearsal room. What is different from the rehearsal to the performance? Adrenaline is often the answer, and perhaps that does play a partial role. However, I propose that it is a heightened state of awareness—a state of awareness of self and the relationship of self to others—that allows music to speak with a clearer voice at that moment and during those times. I believe this is a powerful analogy that can be used to understand the role that awareness plays in the musical and human life of a musician.

Think for a moment of the feeling you get when you are on stage. There is an unbelievable sense of awareness about oneself at *all* times. You are aware of every step, every word, and every physical move. You are constantly aware of everything you do with body, mind, and voice. All seem to work in miraculous coordination that is powerful and transforming. That awareness also provides an immense amount of "feel good" emotion or feedback. Most of us yearn for that aware state (or "performance") because of the feeling it provides and the way in which it seemingly enriches our lives.

For some reason, however, I do not think we have taken enough time to understand that what we are experiencing is a heightened state of awareness of self and others. We associate those feelings and label them as "performance," only attainable in a "performance situation." In fact, we have never been told that what we learn as musicians with respect to awareness can and should be transferred to our everyday lives, which is not only possible but also relatively easy to attain. It is a simple transfer. It is a simple act of knowing when one is unaware and aware. It is a simple matter of knowing when one is awake or in a state of wakefulness, or in a state of unawareness. Unawareness has a dulling, numbing feeling.

Unfortunately, many of us live our musical lives—and, even more unfortunately, our day-to-day lives—"off stage" in the shadows, similar to being off stage at a performance. We teach and conduct rehearsals in the shadows of awareness. We continue to inhabit those shadowy offstage places as we deal with colleagues and other musicians with whom we are attempting to interact. We never operate in a radiant illumination. We don't perceive ourselves as being illuminated. Many of us are never fully illuminated in the face of others. That is a simple matter of self-perception.

I have learned a great deal in past years about somatics and the power of a Body Map from the teachings of Barbara Conable. Simply stated, if our mental map of our body is correct, then we will, in turn,

perceive our body in the correct way, and physical usage of the body (especially as musicians) dramatically improves. I am convinced that the principle of Body Mapping can be applied to a mapping of one's awareness. It is a process of understanding what it is to be musical while concurrently in the "awareness light"—in other words, making music while being on life's stage, in full illumination, fully aware and vital at all times.

Great composers, I believe, somehow know this total state of awareness. Someone once posed the following question to Robert Shaw: "Do you not believe, Mr. Shaw, that the 'Crucifixius' of the *B Minor Mass* of Bach is the greatest musical depiction of the crucifixion of Christ known to music?" Mr. Shaw replied, in effect, that the "Crucifixius" of the *B Minor Mass* is not programmatic. What makes that music so profound is that Bach understood the enormity of the event and its effect upon all of humankind. What Bach brought to that piece and every piece he wrote was an awareness of the world and of life. No one would argue Johannes Brahms' unique viewpoint of life—that is, the ability of his music, in a type of aware melancholia, to be able to look backward in life and see with a sharp awareness the complexity of human existence. Both composers must have written while in a state of incredible awareness of not only themselves, but also the human condition they constantly inhabited. Benjamin Britten began his days with an ice cold bath. He often said that such a bath made him start his day more aware and in touch with the world!

Many of us make mistakes during our "walk" because we drift unknowingly between an illuminated life and a life in the shadows. When we operate in the shadows, we will make many errors because of our unawareness. We hurt others while in these shadows, we hurt students while in these shadows, and we invariably hurt those we love, respect, and admire simply because we are unaware. We have no Body Map of awareness, and if we have no Body Map of awareness, then it is impossible to perceive the brilliance of our aware and conscious self.

We must teach ourselves to heighten our own self-attentive levels. We must map our consciousness to include the feelings of the illumined life that are able to be aware of self, aware of others, and aware of our body. All three interact to move us into the light that is brilliant awareness. On our walk, it is best to start the journey when we are young, understanding this awareness. I believe such brilliant awareness will eliminate the terrible human stumbling we all have experienced that manifests itself by hurting others in some way, where the scapegoat is always "the music." Awareness of self and others must be our constant state of consciousness for any music to be made. Music made in the shadows of unawareness of our own human condition and place in the world will never be brilliant and resplendent. When I hear people remark that a performance was

technically amazing but "no music was made," this is a situation
where the motivating force in evoking the music was operating in a
state of unawareness.

Think of what it is to operate in the brilliant lights of a stage. Map
your consciousness, and recall the times when you have been in such
a state of heightened awareness and self-perception when you were
performing. Struggle daily to maintain such an aware "cognitive map"
—an awareness of life. Not only will your music be transformed and
be placed in a luminous field, but you will also see others with whom
you have contact in a more brilliant, loving, and caring way. Be in an
awake state at all times; be in the light....

"How can we ever accomplish all that we are required to do as musician

"The Way Left"

Chapter 3

The Walk: One Step at a Time

My experiences are nothing special, just ordinary human ones. (p. 1)

Tenzin Gyatso, The Fourteenth Dalai Lama
The Compassionate Life

There are moments in our lives, there are moments in a day, when we seem to see beyond the usual. Such are the moments of our greatest happiness. Such are the moments of our greatest wisdom. If one could but recall his vision by some sort of sign. It was in this hope that the arts were invented. Sign posts on the way to what may be. Sign posts toward greater knowledge. (p. 13)

For an artist to be interesting to us he must have been interesting to himself. He must have been capable of intense feeling, and capable of profound contemplation. (p. 17)

Robert Henri
The Art Spirit

26

Spiritual emptiness is not only an open mind but also an open self. We have to get ourselves out of the way—our explanations, our goals, our habits, and our anxieties. We often try to avoid disaster and fill life with order and meaning, but just as often life unravels all our careful preparations. (p. 10)

Psychologically, emptiness is the absence of neurosis, which is essentially an interfering with the unfolding of life and the desires of the deep soul. Various neuroses, such as jealously, inferiority, and narcissism, are nothing more than anxious attempts to prevent life from happening, and when emptied, they transform into their opposites: Jealousy empty of ego is passion. Inferiority empty of ego is humility. Narcissism empty of ego is love of one's soul. We could understand our struggles with these emotions as an invitation to emptiness. The point is not to get rid of them but to let them get rid of us. (pp. 13–14)

Thomas Moore

T h e   S o u l ' s   R e l i g i o n

These things will destroy the human race:
    politics without principle,
    progress without compassion,
    wealth without work,
    learning without silence,
    religion without fearlessness, and
    worship without awareness.

Anthony de Mello, S.J.

ᴚlɐW s'uɐiɔisuM ǝdT

Thus, the story of Adam and Eve is not about sin, disobedience, sex,
or shame, but is an attempt to explain the reality of death. The first
lesson in this tradition having to do with living the good life is that
life, however good, is finite, a limited resource, and that one does not
have all the time in the world to discover what it is or how to live it.
The first duty of self-awareness, therefore, is the knowledge of the
fewness of one's days. (p. 136)

Peter J. Gomes
The Good Life

Man sees things that surround him long before he becomes aware of
his own self. Many of us are conscious of the hiddenness of things,
but few of us sense the mystery of our own presence. (p. 61)

Abraham Joshua Heschel
Between God and Man

Years of being a counselor have enormously increased my suspicion
of both guilt and loneliness. I know guilt is hell and that guilty people
therefore are deserving of much sympathy. But what I am beginning
to suspect is that most guilty people reject the possibility of
forgiveness not because it is too good to believe, but because they fear
the responsibility forgiveness entails. It's hell to be guilty, but it's
worse to be responsible. (p. 18)

William Sloane Coffin
Credo

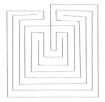

28

The elders told us that this is the road of life that we're walking down. We're supposed to be holding up one another, supporting each other, having our arm beneath our brother's arms while walking down the road of life. (p. i)

Reuben Snake

"Winnebago Medicine Man"

The Way Things Are by Huston Smith

If we are to understand the phenomena of nature, or the qualities of human beings, or the relationship of God or to some different, spiritual experience, we can learn much through music. Music is so very important and interesting to me because it is at the same time everything and nothing. If you wish to learn how to live in a democratic society, then you would do well to play in an orchestra. For when you do, you know when to lead and when to follow. You leave space for others and at the same time you have no inhibitions about claiming a space for yourself. And despite this, or maybe precisely because of it, music is the best means of escape from the problems of human existence. (p. 173)

Daniel Barenboim

Parallels   and   Paradoxes

Birth is a beginning and death is a destination.
And life is a journey:
From childhood to maturity
And youth to age;
From innocence to awareness
And ignorance to knowing;
From foolishness to discretion
And then, perhaps, to wisdom;

The Musician's Walk

From weakness to strength
Or strength to weakness
And, often, back again;
From health to sickness
And back, we pray, to health again;
From offense to forgiveness,
From loneliness to love,
From joy to gratitude,
From pain to compassion,
And grief to understanding.
From fear to faith;
From defeat to defeat to defeat
Until, looking backward or ahead,
We see that victory lies
Not at some high place along the way,
But in having made the journey, stage by stage,
A sacred pilgrimage.
Birth is a beginning
And death is a destination and life is a journey,
A sacred pilgrimage to life everlasting.

Yom Kippur Prayer

We lose too much of essential human qualities in the civilizing process. We are a web of inhibitions...And a musician must be one to whom something is more important than himself.

One of the most beautiful stories I know concerns a certain African tribe in which, at the time when the boy passes into manhood he must go off into the jungle by himself—there to indulge in an orgy of dancing and shouting and wailing and sobbing. He must leave the village—for his sounds would make the people in the village ill.

30

Kathleen Ferriers and Eileen Farrells and Toscaninis and Walters are great because they find the basic and, finally, simple human sound in what for the rest of us are mazes of complexity. (p. 346)

Robert Shaw

The Robert Shaw Reader by Robert Blocker

So we decide for some reason to become a musician. Some of us decide to be performers; some decide to be teachers, conductors, music therapists, theorists, or historians. We decide our genre: choral, instrumental, or classroom. We decide to teach children, high school students, or college students, or to go it alone as a performer. These decisions are all initially based on where we feel most comfortable and at ease. We seek out training either privately or at institutions that can help us achieve our dreams. For many of us, what we do now at this point in our lives is different from our initial dreaming. For example, all I wanted to be was a high school band director. My life course and loves have dramatically changed my career direction.

But amid all the instruction and all the training, few, if any, words of advice (let alone a course instruction) deal with the most central aspects of all our careers: how the people we work with and come in contact with profoundly affect our lives and our music.

The Musician's Walk

In fact, apart from learning the art, there is nothing more important than understanding the alchemy between and among music and people. We have all been shortchanged in our education. No one dares to talk about the "how to" of fostering relationships with those with whom we work and, most importantly, with ourselves. We are given few, if any, tools to balance the art of music making with human ego.

Because music is such a personal art, musicians tend to use the art form as both a shield and a defense for inhumane behavior toward others. They use music as a scapegoat for treating others with disrespect and lack of professionalism. When trying to justify a guilty conscience for aggressive behavior toward someone, musicians ameliorate their guilt by hiding behind the music—the art can justify all.

On the human stage, however, the art cannot justify all, and music suffers because of such attitudes. The phrase is often used that "art reflects life." If musicians have the objectivity to hear their art, they will find that the music they make is directly proportional to the love and care they exercise in their daily comings and goings. Many persons who are given great musical gifts are, perhaps, the greatest offenders. They disregard the feelings of others because they know they are good musicians. But it is those people who do not listen closely to the music they make, for if they do, they would hear in sound the reflections of their ways.

I have wondered why our profession has not given more attention to the care and nurturing of all of us with regard to an ethical code that would help guide us through this thicket. We fill college catalogs with coursework in skill development and methods, but nowhere have I seen a course entitled "Ethics and the Musician."

Music performance and music education have suffered because we have not had the sense as a profession (at least corporately) to value human relationships on the same level as our art. Far too much time has been spent on music technique and not enough on the musicians themselves. Neglect of the musicians, of their inner spirits, and the things that make them human and alive profoundly affect their music making.

It should be no mystery: Music is made with people. Great programs are made with the help of dedicated colleagues, but neither music nor programs of great instruction are possible without understanding and care of human beings. Many musicians "talk the talk" but simply do not "walk the walk." They act as if they care for people but exhibit self-centered and cruel behavior at every turn. I overheard a conductor say he knew of many people who made great music but were not very nice people. "You don't need one to have the other," he remarked. I couldn't disagree more. While music—and especially music education—has advanced in methodology over the years, it has remained relatively prehistoric in its approach to equipping its professionals with necessary and important life tools

that grow not only musicians, but people.

A cautionary word: There are people who because of some gift (whether it is their upbringing, emotional make-up, or spiritual core) do all the right things all the time; they are one of life's joys to be around. I had the rare privilege of sharing my first job with such a person. We were approximately forty years apart in age. It is only after some twenty-five years that I realize what an incredible colleague and teacher this person was. He certainly was a great musician, but he was a greater human being—kind, caring, fair, compassionate, *humble,* and quiet, yet strong. He forced me into another way of thinking and caring while I taught. At the time, I could not figure out why he was able to make such great music, but I think I now have a glimmering.

Great teachers in any subject matter have one unifying characteristic: they are at all times caring and loving to *all* whom they teach or work with, including themselves. They have respect for others and what they do, and they learn from others by quiet observance. They have the unique ability to be able to rejoice in the achievements of others while objectively looking at their own achievements and realizing their own gifts, too. They have an overriding passion for care and human condition of others. Their subject matter is almost an afterthought. Because of these characteristics, students under their tutelage grow at alarming rates both as musicians and people.

I was recently taken aback at a conference where I gave the keynote address. After my address, there was a one-act play. About ten minutes into the play, I realized that it engendered to put the content of my two previous books, *The Musician's Soul* (GIA, 1999) and *The Musician's Spirit* (GIA, 2002), into a theater piece. The incredibly gifted actor, Sam Gilliam, was able to bring alive my words. A significant portion of the play was devoted to understanding what *passion* was. It was the conclusion of that play, however, that had the most profound impact on all of us there.

How can we ever accomplish all that we are required to do as musicians? How can we balance this thing we call passion with human relationships, love, and care? Her answer: "One step at a time."

So this book is about each one of those steps—not the musical steps, but the human steps. What steps must we take to ensure our journeys are as joyful and rewarding as they should be? Our careers are truly built one step at a time. It takes time, however, to try to understand the true nature of what the musician's walk entails, step to step. Mere direction is insufficient. We must have enough information to plot the path of each step so our professional lives can be reflected in the music we make.

The musician's walk…we walk, one step at a time.

"They exist in a lonely world where all they know is music."

"Proud Totem"

Chapter 4

The Loneliness of Musicians: Breeding Unawareness

Seriously religious people and genuine artists sometimes live out there on the outskirts of reason. They have their mystical moments and their true inspirations. They know they have to be half in this world and half in another, just to do their work. Yes, they teeter on the edge of real insanity, but generally they walk the border and have the benefits of a threshold existence. (p. 262)

Thomas Moore
Dark Nights of the Soul

There are times when music educators are lonely people. I think this is sometimes self-inflicted. However, we do teach a different language. We exist in isolated parts of the building because we "make noise." We may have an itinerant assignment in which we are only in the building for a short period of time. Sometimes we do not want to have relationships with those who are not supportive of us or our programs, but is essential that we attempt to do so.

Kenneth R. Raessler

38

Ill hath he chosen his part who seeks to please
The worthless world—ill hath he chosen his part,
For often he must wear the look of ease
When grief is in his heart;
And often in his hours of happier feeling
With sorrow must his countenance be hung,
And ever his own better thoughts concealing
Must he in stupid Grandeur's praise be loud,
And the errors of the ignorant crowd
Assent with lying tongue.

Michelangelo

The Life of Michelangelo Buonarroti (1807)

In the late nineteenth century, the great psychologist William James, through both objective research and philosophical inquiry, noticed that things change the more a person attends to or "concentrates" on them. In essence, the more people believe that they are "focusing," or concentrating, the more they become unaware. It has been my observation that musicians believe—and, in many cases, have been taught—that such focusing and concentration skills will bring a heightened awareness and, hence, a higher level of music making. Unfortunately, this could not be farther from the truth.

If you asked most musicians whether they considered themselves to be aware human beings, they would likely, without hesitation, reply

The Musician's Walk

"yes." Considering their immediate musical world, they probably are somewhat aware of the music and the process of making that music; however, the reality is that because they "focus" so intensively on the music, they begin to create a vast unawareness of the world, their environment and, most importantly, other human beings. Their world of reality is defined by their perceived "connection" to the music. The sad fact is that they may be connected to the sound in some way, but they are hopelessly disconnected from the world. It is the connection to the world that fuels great music making and imbues the music with qualities of honesty, integrity, and depth. It is possible to make music at a somewhat high level with what I will call "unaware focus of attention." However, if one would really listen in a profound way, one would hear a certain type of hollowness and hard quality to the music making. Spontaneity is present, but it is a peculiar spontaneity characterized by tension and lack of freedom in the sound, whether vocal or instrumental. Ellen Langer in her book, *The Power of Mindful Learning,* coins the term for all-inclusive awareness as "soft vigilance" (p. 43).

Soft vigilance is the ability to be aware at all times of all things. Awareness of body and self is paramount: awareness of self in relation to the world and awareness of the constant human connection necessary in the music making process, a tethering to other human beings that is bound by love and care for each other *while music is being made* and, most importantly, *after the music stops.* Such constant soft vigilance must be the goal for all of us twenty-four hours a day, seven days a week. Some of these vigilance issues will be addressed in Chapter 6: "I and Thee."

For too many musicians, there is a naive and unknowing separation between how they live while making music and how they live when they are not. (I am not referring to big moral issues, but rather smaller ones.) It *is* a question of awareness. The vigilance of being aware should not change when one is making music and when one is not; yet it does for many of us. What is optimal is when we can walk into rehearsal and not feel a need to "morph" our human selves into a different being that is necessary for making music. I am sure we all know of people in our lives who do this. They are able to make music at certain high levels and inspire students in the classroom, but their being radically changes when they have to deal with people; they often become gruff and angular with others, although they don't perceive it. And the reason they don't perceive it is because they are *not aware.* These people are "fulfilled" when making music but are vapidly empty and unaware as they move through their lives. They tend to become angry and defend their anger to themselves as necessary because they do it "for music." But music was never intended to be a vehicle that justifies inhumanity toward others. Such musicians and artists, in general, experience this highly unique type of loneliness. Ironically, this loneliness is difficult to perceive. It is felt rather than experienced. The loneliness is tolerated because of the joys that music making provides. Music making unknowingly acts as a soothing balm for the soul. Meanwhile, these music makers have no guilt about their relationships with the world around them. At times, they exist in a lonely world where all they know is music, and they divorce that music from the life they experience day to day. They are aware of music but unaware of themselves and the world in which they exist.

The marriage of music making and life, or the ability to have "work" and "play" be as one in life, is the challenge. We are unaware, and we are brilliantly aware. We should strive to be brilliantly aware through the constancy of this miracle of soft vigilance. This excerpt from a Robert Frost poem states it beautifully:

But yield who will to their separation,
My object in living is to unite
My avocation and my vocation
As my two eyes make one in sight.
Only where love and need are one,
And the work is play for mortal stakes
Is the deed ever really done
For Heaven and the future's sakes.

Robert Frost
Two Tramps in Mud Time

"Compassion must exist for music to have its truest voice."

"Kachina Mother"

Chapter 5

The Compassionate Musician

Most of us, it seems to me, *want to be made use of.* We want whatever intuitive talent we have, whatever intelligence we've accumulated, whatever energies our genes and the Great Unknown have provided—to be used.

That's one of the reasons we're in this volunteer chorus together. (It may be the main reason. Well, let me tell you very frankly that I also come to Monday evening rehearsals as a volunteer. To my way of thinking, this only makes Monday nights more important. We're obviously the ones who care. (pp. 240–241)

Robert Shaw

Dear People... by Joseph Mussulman

We cannot do great things, but we can do small things with great love.

Mother Teresa

44   Ultimately, the reason why love and compassion bring the greatest happiness is simply that our nature cherishes them above all else. However capable and skillful an individual may be, left alone, he or she will not survive. However vigorous and independent we may feel during the most prosperous periods of life, when we are sick, or very young or very old, we depend on the support of others. (p. 8)

Even in ordinary conversation in everyday life, when someone speaks with warm human feeling, we enjoy listening and respond accordingly; the whole conversation becomes interesting, however unimportant the topic may be. On the other hand, if a person speaks coldly or harshly, we feel uneasy and wish for a quick end to the interaction. From the least important to the most important event, the affection and respect of others are vital for our happiness. (p. 10)

As human beings we all have the potential to be happy and compassionate people, and we also have the potential to be miserable and harmful to others. (p. 11)

Thus, we not only need compassion and human affection to survive, but they are the ultimate sources of success in life. Selfish ways of thinking not only harm others, they prevent the very happiness we ourselves desire. The time has come to think more wisely, hasn't it? (p. 15)

Self-centeredness inhibits our love for others, and we are all afflicted by it to one degree or another. For true happiness to come about, we need a calm mind, and such peace of mind is brought about only by a compassionate attitude. How can we develop this attitude? Obviously, it is not enough for us simply to believe that compassion is important and to think about how nice it is! We need to make a concerted effort to develop it; we must use all the events of our daily life to transform our thoughts and behavior. (p. 20)

Tenzin Gyatso, The Fourteenth Dalai Lama
The Compassionate Life

Needless to say, what is in particular that we care about has a considerable bearing upon the character and quality of our lives. It makes a great difference that certain things and not others are important to us. But the very fact that there are things that we care about—that we do care about something—is even more fundamentally significant. The reason is that this fact bears not just upon the individual specificity of a person's life, but upon its basic structure. Caring is indispensably foundational as an activity that connects and binds us to ourselves. (p. 17)

Love makes it possible, in other words, for us to engage wholeheartedly in activity that is meaningful. Insofar as self-love is tantamount just to a desire to love, it is simply a desire to be able to count on having meaning in our lives. (p. 90)

Harry Frankfurt
The Reasons of Love

It may come as no great surprise that interaction with the environment can alter our mental architecture. But there is also accumulating evidence that the brain can change autonomously, in response to its own internal signals. Last year, Tibetan Buddhist Monks, with the encouragement of the Dalai Lama, submitted to functional magnetic resonance imaging as they practiced

46   "compassion meditation," which is aimed at achieving a mental state
of pure loving-kindness toward all beings. The brain scans only
showed a slight effect in novice meditators. But for monks who had
spent more than ten thousand hours in meditation, the differences in
brain function were striking. Activity in the left prefrontal cortex, the
locus of joy, overwhelmed activity in the right prefrontal cortex, the
locus of anxiety. Activity was also heightened in the areas of the brain
that directly planned motion, "as if all monks' brains were itching to
go to the aid of those in distress," Sharon Begley reported in the *Wall
Street Journal.* All of which suggests, say the scientists who carried
out the scans, that "the resting state of the brain may be altered by
long-term meditative practice." (p. 13)

Jim Holt
"Of Two Minds"
The New York Times Magazine

There are two words, "compassionate" and "musician" (also
"compassionate" and "educator"), that do not seem to be commonly
associated with each other on a regular basis. In either case, a union
of these two important words should be commonplace, but it seems
to have somehow escaped the consciousness and awareness of us all.
Moreover, it would seem that this semantic marriage should be
somewhat omnipresent in our minds.

However, I think we would be hard pressed to locate these words in educational philosophy, method, or conducting books. Compassion is one of the qualities that I believe all truly great human beings possess. Persons who do great things and small things define compassion by example and deed. Compassion also seems to be a state of being rather than an act: One does not solely do compassionate things, but rather one's being is compassionate. This is an important distinction that, once understood, will transform the message of what music carries. I would like to explore the nature of compassion and make a meager attempt at defining its boundaries and its role in the music making process.

In the summer of 2003, the Dalai Lama was speaking in Central Park. Mostly out of curiosity, I journeyed to the city. I arrived at Central Park along with hundreds of thousands of others! I stood in line for two hours and finally made my way onto the Great Green.

Thousands stood, sat, and kneeled in absolute silence—a throng of diverse human beings that were drawn together to hear a message. The Dalai Lama had been speaking for approximately one-half hour when I entered the Green. The first thing I heard, which was met with tumultuous applause, was the following statement by the Dalai Lama (a paraphrase from my memory):

"It seems to me that the most important thing we can teach our children and each other is compassion. Compassion should be our curriculum."

I stood for a few minutes a bit dazed. The word was not revolutionary, but the idea struck me as revolutionary. I must confess that in all I have taught and experienced in music education, and all I have experienced as a conductor, I had never given much thought to compassion. Compassion, I thought, had not been in my awareness. Why? The more I thought, the more I realized that while I understood the gestalt of compassion, I couldn't immediately grasp the many dimensions of human compassion. I understood its definition, but I could not translate the word via human acts or human feelings. I tried to define it and could only arrive at a general synonym that paralleled an overall meaning of the word.

I am now not sure I ever understood this incredible word. Moreover, I don't believe it has been in the conscious forefront of my music making, teaching, or general life awareness. Basically and bluntly stated, I discovered that I was not aware of compassion. Or rather, an awareness of compassion was not an integral part of my conscious life. It took the words of a holy man to force me to hear that message.

The Musician's Walk

First of all, we must be clear what we mean by *compassion*. Many forms of compassionate feeling are mixed with desire and attachment. For instance, the love parents feel for their child is often strongly associated with their own emotional needs, so it is fully compassionate. Usually when we are concerned about a close friend, we call this compassion, but it too is usually attachment.

Compassion without attachment is possible. Therefore, we need to clarify the distinctions between compassion and attachment. True compassion is not just an emotional response but a firm commitment founded on reason. (pp. 20–21)

Tenzin Gyatso, The Fourteenth Dalai Lama
The Compassionate Life

compassionate awareness

Part of the unconscious human condition is compassionate. But compassion is not in our aware and conscious life. We are in a state of compassionate unawareness when we are making music—not deliberately, but rather from a state of ignorance.

The quote above has helped me to understand compassion. If asked whether they were "compassionate," most musicians would invariably answer "yes." However, what we label as compassion is, in reality, an attachment. This attachment is through the music to people. When we conduct or teach, we are experiencing a particular type of attachment, or connection. Connection is not compassion.

50   Connection can be defined as a communication between people that, in most cases, is based upon the *needs* of each of the parties involved. The needs and wants of the ensemble and of the human beings experiencing music are real. Their spiritual expectations, conscious or unconscious, are legitimate expectations; however, the problem lies with the teacher/conductor in this process.

A compassionate "state" exists during rehearsal and performance when the needs of others, not ourselves, are omnipresent in the space. Stated another way, we the teachers or we the conductors are not important. To be in a compassionate state, our own personal wants must be absent so we can clearly see and feel the needs of others. Some would also refer to the strong will that accompanies those needs in a conductor or teacher as "ego."

Musicians, who occupy the role of chief "evoker" in a musical situation, cannot bring ego into the room. Yet many musicians do so on a regular basis. They talk about connection with their ensembles, and even through the sheer force of their personalities, they literally "will" the music to life. Such music making tends to be typified by the hallmarks of "exciting" and "rhythmic," but a look beneath the surface reveals an atmosphere that is restrictive and controlled. Attachments to the ensemble are thrust upon the ensemble. What is ultimately desirable is for conductors to understand that by making themselves

The Musician's Walk

less, the ensemble becomes more—more musically and more spiritually. Over time, will and ego are ultimately dehumanizing. Moreover, such psychological oppression will never allow for a compassionate atmosphere to be born in the classroom or the rehearsal room. Ego, or the constant presence of "I," will inhibit compassion.

So this discussion focuses on the awareness and importance of others. To open the channels of compassion, the teacher/evoker must possess humbleness as music is being taught and created, and must practice humbleness even in the face of adversity. Understand that a musical challenge—the inability to sing accurately in tune or the ability to sing a correct rhythm—is a sound representation or symbolism of struggles in life. For those of us who have faced such profound and life-changing struggles, there is one characteristic that seems to bind blood to bone. Faced with life's ultimate challenges, love and the importance of others becomes paramount. When this state exists, the feeling in the air is one of compassion. Compassion must exist for music to have its truest voice—its most life-altering voice.

If anger exists in any form, then music cannot be born. If overpowering ego exists, then music cannot speak. If love does not exist in the room, then human spirits cannot be present. The road to such a compassionate state is developed, just as mimetics instructs us

52 (*The Musician's Soul*, 1999), through conscious and constant effort. An identification of favorable conditions is the initial awareness, which must be defined. A type of mastery of mindfulness and awareness must be in constant cultivation within oneself. For this to occur, you must be *less* so that you can be truly aware of the others in the room who are struggling to make music because you are in the way. Compassion is present when others and their life needs are important, and you feel them and know them.

Compassion is one of the ultimate awarenesses of life, which should be at the center of all that we do. By its very nature, music in some way, shape, or form carries a message in sound of the compassionate human state. If one does not struggle to *be* compassionate and live compassionately, then music and the souls who perform it will never revel in its glory or its message. It is that message which is music's gift.

"Immediacy and intimacy of human relationships
is central to music making."

"Nestled Sphere"

Chapter 6

I and Thee

This is It

And I am It

And You are It

And so is

That

And He is It

And She is It

And It is It

And That is That.

O It is This

And It is Thus

And It is Them

And It is Us

And It is Now

And here It is

And here We are

So This is It. (p. 374)

James Broughton

Life Prayers by Elizabeth Roberts

56

The title of this chapter is a bit of a play on words. "I and Thee" has a striking similarity to the title of the translation of the book by Martin Buber titled *I and Thou*. The substitution of the word "thee" is a play on the use of the pronoun "thee" that is substituted by Quakers for the more commonly used pronoun "you." Both the phrase and the pronoun substitution, when combined, form a powerful paradigm for forging lasting and meaningful relationships with persons who make music together.

Running the risk of oversimplification in Buber's book, the phrase "I and thou" is used to represent the intimate human relationship between two human beings or a group of human beings. Loosely interpreted, "I and thou" are one and the same. To understand "thou," one must believe that "I" and "thou" are one with each other. The Quakers' use of "thee" instead of "you" is used in speech and writing in a similar way. "Thee" is used to personalize "I"—that is, "I" and "thee" are the same person sharing the same earth, air, space, hopes, and desires. You are not "you," but rather "thee." "Thee" is more sacred and personal than "you." The use of "thee" also assumes that you (or I) are bound to the other.

"I and Thee" accurately and beautifully describes the relationship of those persons who make music with each other, whether it be the members of a string quartet or the 180 members of a choir. For any humanly meaningful communication to take place, a visual paradigm needs to be put in place.

What is your relationship to your ensemble? Do you view them as 180 separate chorus members, or do you view the chorus as the corporate body, a blur of humanity that contains 180 bodies? The use of the phrase "I and thee" is meant to suggest the paradigm in which you view yourself as a conductor or teacher being connected directly to each person in the ensemble with a type of human umbilical cord or tether. As you conduct or teach, the temporal distance is closed between you and each member of the ensemble through a shortening of that imaginary but very real philosophical tenure. Your connection to each person in the room is 1:1 rather than 1:180. Unless you view yourself in such a way, communication, let alone any type of human connection, is virtually impossible.

Immediacy and intimacy of human relationships is central to music making. People sing and play in ensembles first because such a relationship exists. They don't know what it is that draws them to that ensemble, but they sense that their spirits are fed. When "I and thee" exists in a rehearsal, the basic fundamental ingredient for musical line and good pitch is present: the need for relationship with another human being.

n a b ɿ o ſ   ꙅ ɘ m a ſ

58

Let's go outside of music for an illustration. I was speaking to someone on a past anniversary of the September 11 terrorist attack on the World Trade Center who worked in close proximity to those buildings, who was evacuating his building just after the second plane struck. I asked him what his most overriding vision of that day is.

He responded by saying that it was difficult for him to talk about it, but that he had spent much time thinking not only about moments frozen in his mind but also about the meaning of those frozen moments. He relayed to me how he was unable to forget the sight as he looked upward at the wounded buildings to see human beings leaping from the buildings. He remembers in nightmares a stunningly beautiful moment amidst the human horror of that morning: He saw two people leaping from different sections of tower two. As they were falling to the ground, each to their chosen fate, somehow they saw each other and reached out for one another. Seemingly God drew their bodies together in free fall, and they grasped hands and fell to their death.

My friend remarked at how, ironically, that recurring image has refocused his life. "Imagine," he remarked, "that in the last moments of two lives, their overwhelming need was for connection to each other by the warmth of their clenched hands. All that mattered at the end of their lives was to be connected with another human being." I thought at the time that this was "I and thou," as Buber envisioned it.

But perhaps even more personal, it is "I and thee."

"I and thee" is a basic human need that making music can fulfill providing the teacher/conductor understands that the need for such connection is real and necessary not only for music making, but also for human existence. For many, when these connections are few and far between in life, making music can provide "I and thee" moments that enrich their life. Ensemble conductors and teachers of music must ensure that the "I and thee" are always present in all they do, say and, most importantly, be.

How to *be* as one teaches music or performs music is *the* most important aspect to making music with others. Nothing else is as important. I know many persons who can and do make music without the presence of "I and thee." There is something hollow about the sound which, I believe, is because of the lack of human resonance, the kind of resonances that can only be generated between people.

My mother recently passed away after a long battle with cancer. It was difficult for me. I felt helpless and awkward. One day near the end of her life, she said, "You know, Jim, when you get really ill, you find out who your friends really are. And it is a bit ironic, but I really need people with me now, and some never come." In her remaining days, I watched as her life friends came and sat, and they sat silently, as did I, holding her hand. The only medicine that mattered was human

60   touch and the electricity of human compassion and love. On the day she passed, her only surviving brother, eighty-seven years young, who she adored, came ten minutes before her passing. My Mom adored her brother. They were life's friends. He sat down, held her hand, and she passed quietly and beautifully.

"I and thee" again. It is often said that art mirrors life. I am fearful that this basic human component in music making and life is left unnoticed by so many. "I and thee" should be at the core of everyone's demeanor and humanity in rehearsal.

Since my Mom's passing and since my friend's 9/11 experiences were shared, I stand in front of ensembles a bit differently. Every time my hands are raised to begin, I think of my hands holding each hand in the room. I am filled with a warmth and love that, I believe, allows music to speak with a powerful and profound voice. It is this relationship in the musician's walk that can empower all of us.

"...understand that this is not a reflection of their spirits."

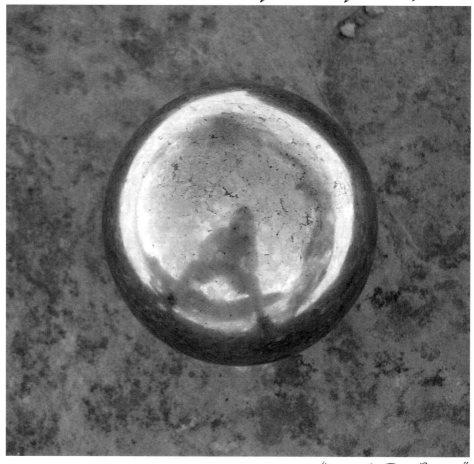

"Reflected Sphere"

Chapter 7

Who Am I? Who Are They? Confusion Between Human Self and Musical Self

Psychologically speaking, there is something particularly naked about actually being your own instrument. No other musician deals with this exact situation. I find it interesting that pianists tend to argue more vehemently than any other instrumentalists that singers have "no excuse" for their behavior. I believe it is because pianists are the only musicians who do not perform exclusively on their own instruments. Most other musicians travel with their own instruments. If the instrument malfunctions, the musician may have it repaired or, if necessary, replaced. Pianists must learn the intricacies of a new instrument in every concert venue, often with limited rehearsal time. In both cases, however, the instrument is external to the person using it, and its tonal characteristics are not considered synonymous with the musician himself.

Many singers deal with the problem of separating themselves from "the voice." Dozens of singers I know will describe the actions of "the voice" as completely alien to their own desires, as though "the voice" itself were another person misbehaving in their relationship in an attempt to force separation. The blurred line between the voice and the true self leads to enormous highs and lows. When the instrument is you and your performance receives thunderous applause, the high is tremendous. The "off" nights, on the other hand, can't simply be left onstage. One student told me she holds back when she sings because of her fear that if someone doesn't like the sound of her voice, she "can't go out and buy a new one." If she doesn't allow the true sound of her voice to be heard, I reminded her, she will not receive encouragement from others, and she will trap herself in a chicken-versus-egg conundrum. (pp. 4–5)

Lynn Eustis

The Singer's Ego

So "masked and armored," it turns out, is *not* the safe and sane way to live. If our roles were more deeply informed by the truth that is in our souls, the general level of sanity and safety would rise dramatically. A teacher who shares his or her identity with students is more effective than one who lobs factoids at them from behind a wall. (p. 17)

Parker J. Palmer

A Hidden Wholeness

The Musician's Walk

In preparing to write a foreword for *The Singer's Ego* by Lynn Eustis, I was confronted with an idea that I had never given any thought to. Yet it probably, or rather most likely, has played a rather predominant role in my walk as a conductor and one who works with singers in choirs. If you consider for a moment that there might be some confusion lurking not only in your ensemble but within yourself as to where your sound as a singer (or the sound of your choir) stops and you begin, you will see the groundwork for some inevitable human disasters. Unaware of this dilemma, many of us have probably struggled with issues that we related to the music when, in reality, they were issues that were reflective of our own (or our choir's) inability to understand the relationship between our voice, the sound of the choir, and everyone as human beings. Many of us, I fear, exist in a world that blames all musical problems on a mysterious force that is bound to our humanness. Just like our forefathers recognized the need for separation of church and state, maybe we as musicians should strive for separation of musical voice and human self. In fact, to strive is not sufficient. This should be at the core of our musical training. When we can fully separate the "ego" or "self" from our very connected voice and choral instrument, then real music will be born.

66

Understanding the psychological dilemma singers and choirs face because their body is their only instrument is a very real issue. Singers, confused about their musical identity and their human identities, mutilate themselves when the music isn't right. When the choir doesn't sing well, conductors also mutilate themselves because, after all, that sound is an extension of their total humanness.

However, while their sound as singers is obviously connected to the choir members as human beings, their voice is independent of their spirit. On some days, the voice simply doesn't work. The fact that singers are having trouble singing in tune or singing with a particular style of tone has nothing to do with them as human beings. It is a mechanical malfunction, not a human malfunction. Yet many singers consider their voices as being inseparable from them. When they don't sing well, their spirit becomes the victim of self-abuse and feelings of inadequacy.

Conductors must understand that when the choir does not sing well, or is not able to sing well, it is not about them! The reasons for vocal dysfunction are many: illness, fatigue, humidity, diet...the list goes on and on. When a choir doesn't sing well, conductors should certainly do a quick check to make sure all the human elements in the room are correct. But they must also make sure simple vocal malfunction is not at the root of the day's problems.

So what do you do if the choir is having a bad day vocally? Let it
go. Conduct and rehearse with understanding and compassion. Talk
to the choir about the separation of their human selves from their
vocal selves. Put them at ease when things are not right. Insist on
vocal responsibility on their part, but understand that this is not a
reflection of their spirits. Rather, it is simply a day when things aren't
working!

If a conductor fails to be aware of this inherent dichotomy, then
the scapegoat element of mimetics (*The Musician's Soul,* 1999) comes
into play. The conductor will, unknowingly, "vent" these internal
frustrations on the ensemble. Or more likely, the innocent victims will
be those with whom the conductor works or even those with whom
the conductor lives and shares life with on a daily basis. Once again,
an understanding of this voice/human duality coupled with the
mimetic state of constant love and care for self and ensemble will
neutralize this powerful source of deep trouble for both musicians
and conductors.

"...each of us is charged with re-inventing the ethical wheel."

"Infinite Blossom"

Chapter 8

An Ethical Code for Artists Defined by Awareness

As human beings we all have the potential to be happy and compassionate people, and we also have the potential to be miserable and harmful to others.

My main concern is always how to promote an understanding of deeper human value. This deeper human value is compassion, a sense of caring, and commitment. No matter what your religion, and whether you are a believer or a nonbeliever, without them you cannot be happy. (pp. 11–12)

But on a day when our mood is less positive and we are feeling irritated, automatically our inner door closes. As a result, even if we encounter our best friend, we feel uncomfortable and strained. These instances show how our inner attitude makes a great difference in our daily experiences. In order to create a pleasant atmosphere within ourselves, within our families, within our communities, we have to realize that the ultimate source of that pleasant atmosphere is within the individual, within each of us a good heart, human compassion, love. (pp. 12–13)

Tenzin Gyatso, The Fourteenth Dalai Lama

The Compassionate Life

70

The sacrifice of self—that is, the making sacred of the personality naturally leads to a life sensitive to all that is not the self, which is one way to define ethics. (p. 213)

Ethos, from which we get the word *ethics,* originally meant a place where animals frequent. When we herd together, how do we behave? Do we look after one another? Do we take care of the place where we gather—the land, the city, the drinking water? Are we welcome here? Can we be ourselves? These are basic questions of human existence, and how we answer them and live them has everything to do with our ethics. (p. 214)

Ethics is a way of recognizing that although we are each alone in this universe, we are all alone together. We can make a good life not only by protecting each other but by being creative together and taking our pleasures from one another. (pp. 215–216)

Ethics is a form of soul care because it clears away significant obstacles to the movement of life. Conversely, failure in ethics is always a signal of some fundamental anxiety or blind spot about the nature of things. Any effort toward living ethically is a way of caring for the soul, and anyone seriously interested in living a spiritual life might first consider, honestly and deeply, the state of his ethics and the positive call of his conscience. (p. 220)

Thomas Moore

The Soul's Religion

Some people are really showing excitement about the new Millennium, that the new Millennium itself will bring new happy days. I think that's wrong. Unless there is a new Millennium inside, then the new Millennium will not change much—same days and nights, same sun and moon. The important thing is transformation, or new ways of thinking.

Tenzin Gyatso, The Fourteenth Dalai Lama
Ethics for the New Millennium (video)

Or the waterfall, or music heard so deeply
That is not heard at all, but you are the music
While the music lasts. These are only hints and guesses,
Hints followed by guesses; and the rest
Is prayer, observance, discipline, thought and action.
The hint half guessed, the gift half understood, is Incarnation.

T. S. Elliot
Four Quartets 3: The Dry Salvages

Blunt the sharpness.
Untangle the knot,
Soften the glare,
Merge with dust.

Tao Te Ching

72

The quote comes from Proposition 18 in part IV of *The Ethics* and it reads: "...the very first foundation of virtue is the endeavor (conatum) to preserve the individual self, and happiness consists in the human capacity to preserve its self." In Latin the proposition reads...*virtutis fundamentum esse ip sum conatum proprium esse conservandi, et felicitatem in eo consistere, quòd homo suum esse conservare potest.* (p. 170)

As I interpret it, the proposition is a cornerstone for a generous ethical system. It is an affirmation that at the base of whatever rules of behavior we may ask humanity to follow, there is something inalienable: A living organism, known to its owner because the owner's mind has constructed a self, has a natural tendency to preserve its own life; and that same organism's state of optimal functioning, subsumed by the concept of joy, results from the successful endeavor to endure and prevail. (pp. 170–171)

The biological reality of self-preservation leads to virtue because in our inalienable need to maintain ourselves we must, of necessity, help preserve *other* selves. (p. 171)

I interpret Spinoza to mean that the system constructs ethical imperatives based on the presence of mechanisms of self-preservation in each person, but mindful of social and cultural elements as well. (p. 172)

Antonio Damasio
Looking for Spinoza

Not wanting to soul the self or the soul.   73

As artists, we have antennae sensitive to the thoughts and feelings of those around us. We can be chilled by indifference, hurt by lack of consideration, and we can be exhausted and diminished if we are in the company of those who talk down to us or treat us subtly like the identified patient: "Oh, you and your crazy ideas." As artists, we need our crazy ideas, and we need those who don't think they're too crazy. Symphonies and screenplays begin as crazy ideas. So do novels and nocturnes, bronzes and ballets. (p. 111)

Julia Cameron
Walking in This World

Success can make you go one of two ways. It can make you a prima donna, or it can smooth the edges, take away the insecurities, and let the nice things come out. (p. 153)

Barbara Walters
Walking in This World by Julia Cameron

Love is the spirit that motivates the artist's journey...it is a powerful motive in the artist's life. (p. 267)

Eric Maisel
Walking in This World by Julia Cameron

74

Consider the following. We humans are social beings. We come into the world as the result of others' actions. We survive here in dependence on others. Whether we like it or not, there is hardly a moment of our lives when we do not benefit from others' activities. For this reason it is hardly surprising that most of our happiness arises in the context of our relationships with others. Nor is it so remarkable that our greatest joy should come when we are motivated by concern for others. But that is not all. We find that not only do altruistic actions bring about happiness but they also lessen our experience of suffering. Here I am not suggesting that the individual whose actions are motivated by the wish to bring others' happiness necessarily meets with less misfortune than the one who does not. Sickness, old age, mishaps of one sort or another are the same for us all. But the sufferings which undermine our internal peace, anxiety, doubt, disappointment, these things are definitely less. In our concern for others, we worry less about ourselves. When we worry less about ourselves an experience of our own suffering is less intense.

What does this tell us? Firstly, because our every action has a universal dimension, a potential impact on others' happiness, ethics are necessary as a means to ensure that we do not harm others. Secondly, it tells us that genuine happiness consists in those spiritual qualities of love, compassion, patience, tolerance and forgiveness and so on. For it is these which provide both for our happiness and others' happiness.

Tenzin Gyatso, The Fourteenth Dalai Lama
Ethics for the New Millennium

*W*e desperately need an ethical code in our profession.

Not that I am accusing musicians of being unethical. Codes of ethics, by definition, are guidelines, a direction, a path. I have made many mistakes in my musical life—not with the music I made, but in my unawareness of the world around me. I also believe that I am not unique. When I was twenty-two and entering this profession (or better yet, when I was eighteen and learning about the "profession"), it would have been so helpful to my professional life and my life in general for someone (preferably the profession) to share a code of ethics that would serve as both guide and sign post to live a life in music. Why do we continue to provide little or no direction to those beginning this profession? Why are there no "rules" that have been tempered by wisdom and experience that are handed down from generation to generation? It seems to me a bit ridiculous that despite our advanced methodologies and "philosophies" of music education, a code of ethics to guide musicians is non-existent.

As it stands, each of us is charged with re-inventing the ethical wheel. We find out through painful experience and unpleasant situations when we have made a wrong turn. (Cruelty and inhumanity to colleagues and students are somewhat commonplace.) Such "wrong turns" waste valuable energy for life and music making, and detract from the importance of the music itself. These ethical

n a b ɿ o ſ   z ə m a ſ

76   missteps are not intentional, but they do occur because of a lack of awareness of human beings and the fragile nature of human beings.

It is important to understand the entirety of the musician's walk—to understand that this walk is not about ourselves but is really about how we connect with people in our daily lives as we practice our art. We desperately need to construct a code of ethics, first for ourselves and perhaps later for our profession. This code of ethics needs to be constructed with a newfound awareness of others and our impact upon others. That awareness can only be acquired through a conscious and dedicated desire to seek out all aspects of our lives as we engage in the music-making process.

This book will attempt to point out awarenesses and then, at the end, arrive at a vehicle and structure by which such a code of ethics could be constructed. Such a code, when constructed, could clearly chart one's direction for the "walk" and the implications for one's life of music making.

"There must be a secret,"

"In Her Gaze"

Chapter 9

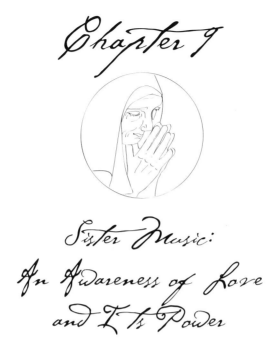

Sister Music: An Awareness of Love and Its Power

What a wonderful thing it would be if once and for all we could lay to rest the notion that it is a virtue to love others and a vice to love oneself. For what is vicious is not self-love but selfishness, and selfishness is more a product of self-hate, than self-love. All forms of selfishness are finally forms of insecurity, compensations for lack of self-love. (p. 21)

William Sloane Coffin
Credo

Good teachers are those people who have gone so deep in their knowledge that they know bitterly and honestly that they don't know. They speak directly from their inability to speak and teach what they know to be unteachable. They may well have found fascinating methods to impart this knowledge beyond knowing, and therefore they tend to be eccentric. If the eccentricity rises up from richness of soul, it is to be trusted, but never naively. For spiritual knowledge in the best of us is always surrounded by potential self-deception and illusion. The good teacher is not afraid of such things and even uses them for the benefit of his students. (pp. 261–262)

Thomas Moore

The S o u l' s   R e l i g i o n

*F*orgive me for telling a story. But sometimes there is nothing that summarizes a difficult point so clearly and with such meaning as a story. As I said in *The Musician's Spirit* (GIA, 2002), stories are all around us. It is almost like they are sent to teach us something we already knew but have refused to acknowledge. Or better yet, stories bring us to a new awareness about life's truths because they are about real people and real life.

Several years ago I was on a working trip to Ireland. A friend of mine there, Blanaid Murphy, had arranged the trip. In addition to working with her choirs, which was the purpose of the trip, she had arranged a number of workshops in and around Dublin to help "pay the bills." It was a hectic week. It seemed like I was workshopping every choir in Dublin.

As the week went on, my schedule seemed to get busier rather than slow down. One day, there were three workshops or clinics, all in different towns. It was nearing the end of my trip and I was a bit tired, yearning for some "down" time.

"We have just one more workshop; it's in Wexford. You know, the town that the Wexford Carol was written for," said Blanaid. In the back of my mind, I tried to figure how I could make it through yet another workshop; they are very demanding. To make matters a bit more difficult, we had to drive about an hour and a half in the pouring rain to get to Wexford.

I never ask beforehand who the prospective audience is. I stay awake worrying about developing an exact workshop agenda; I now find a few hours' notice is all that is necessary. So I asked Blanaid who I would be working with.

"It is a parish school's choir," she said. "They are children from the Catholic parish school there. Quite fine. You must hear them. They are taught by a nun who is a legend around here. They range in age from third grade through ninth grade, boys and girls."

"A parish choir?" I thought. Blanaid is driving me what seemed an interminable distance to work with a parish choir? I was tired and a bit cranky, and this didn't sit well with me at the time. However, I should have known better with Blanaid. She has never led me astray! Unfortunately, I was too tired and cranky to realize that.

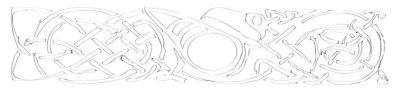

After what seemed an endless drive in the rain, we arrived at the church a few minutes late. I was taken to the back of a church social hall. As I entered the rear of the hall, the room seemed dark. Three electric bulbs hung from cords from the ceiling. Not much light in the room. The room was dark and a bit humid because of the rains.

The social hall was quite deep. Entering from the rear, I could see a group of children sitting patiently and obediently in the front in four rows; the room had an eerie quietness to it. I could hear my footsteps as I walked forward to the choir. When I arrived in front, I was introduced to "Sister."

I do not remember her name, but I will never forget her face. She was at least eighty years of age, probably close to ninety, short, thin, and a bit stoop shouldered. She said a quiet "hello" and "welcome." "We are so glad you are here."

Sister then asked me what I would like to do. I told her I would like to hear the children sing first, and then after hearing them, I would work with them. As I looked at the children, I saw that they had no music. The piano to my left looked unplayable. I wondered what they would possibly be able to sing. I also wondered what kind of an ensemble this was. Children as young as third grade and students as old as ninth grade, all in the same ensemble! I began to imagine the problems I would have to confront.

"May we sing some Palestrina?" asked Sister. I replied, "Yes," and braced myself for the worse. Sister moved to the front of the ensemble and gave a pitch from the rattrap piano. I was standing behind her, so I could not see her face. She began to conduct. I must say that she broke all the "rules" of conducting. I could not make out a gesture—just some minuscule motion that began the piece.

I was breathless. I have never—and I do mean never—heard such a beautiful and honest sound from children. Impeccably in tune, beautiful line...all from memory. In fact, the sound was so beautiful and at the same time so unexpected that I cried. How ironic. In this dark, musty church hall with barely enough light to see came this truly angelic sound.

They ended. Sister turned to me and asked, "Would you like to work with them?" "Yes," I mumbled and thought, "What am I going to teach them?" It was almost perfect. So I searched for a couple of areas to work with them on and chose to address some tempo issues. I told them what a wonderful choir they were and how I would always remember their sound as being one of the most beautiful I had ever heard. I felt that was the best gift I could give them for touching me so deeply and profoundly.

I worked with the children for about an hour. As soon as they were dismissed, I told Blanaid that I must talk with Sister. I wanted to know what she did with these children. "There must be a secret," I thought. Well, there was.

I was reintroduced to Sister again, but this time I felt very humbled to be with her. I told her how much I was touched by the children's singing and asked her to explain what she does with them.

"Well, we sing several times a week together. We have no music, so I teach the parts by rote. One other thing: I teach each student individually in the entire school. From the time they enter the school, they study voice with me during the school day. It is not a lot of time that I can give each one, but I try to use it wisely."

Then I asked the now seemingly foolish question. "What is your secret? What is at the core of your vocal teaching that teaches them such beautiful technique?"

Sister smiled and her octogenarian eyes seemingly smiled at me, and she let out an all knowing "mmmm." I waited for the pearl of wisdom from this obviously gifted and inspired teacher. "I love each one of them," she replied. She said good-bye, thanked me for coming, and walked slowly away.

I have thought much about that afternoon. While I am sure there was a pedagogical path this woman used, it was clear that a spiritually aware and alive human being was the core of this experience for these students. Her faith, I am sure, has brought her through eighty years in a very aware state. She also, probably intuitively, understood the basic need of humans to be loved. And she intimately understood how, through loving, all can be taught.

I was happy I went there that day. I felt a bit foolish for not trusting my friend but was very happy she had "dragged" me there. The trip to Wexford had changed me and had reaffirmed my belief that love of others must be central to all teaching, learning, and sharing. Rather, a constant awareness that love needs to pervade all we do is at the center of any experience.

"True courage is exciting, challenging, stimulating, and truly radiant."

"River Rocks"

Chapter 10

Core vs. Force: A Paradigm for Monitoring the Musician's Walk

Love all Creation

The whole of it and every grain of sand

Love every leaf

Every ray of God's light

Love the animals

Love the plants

Love everything

If you love everything

You will perceive

The divine mystery in things

And once you have perceived it

You will begin to comprehend it ceaselessly

More and more everyday

And you will at last come to love the whole world

With an abiding universal love. (p. 26)

Fyodor Dostoyevsky

Life Prayers by Elizabeth Roberts

88

For our purposes, it's really only necessary to recognize that power is what makes you go strong, while force makes you weak. Love, compassion and forgiveness, which may be mistakenly thought of as submissive by some, are, in fact, profoundly empowering. Revenge, judgementalism and condemnation, on the other hand, inevitably make you go weak. (p. 140)

Individuals of great power throughout human history have been those who have totally aligned themselves with powerful attractors. Again and again, they have stated that the power they manifested was not of themselves. Each has attributed the source of the power to something greater than himself. (p. 141)

In examining these attractors, we'll notice that some weak patterns tend to imitate (in form only) more powerful patterns. These we'll call imitators. Thus, the German people under the Third Reich were deceived by patriotism because they thought it was Patriotism. The demagogue or the zealot tries to sell us imitators as the real thing. Demagogues, to this end, always put forth a great deal of rhetoric...those who move from power need say very little. (p. 141)

On examination, we'll see that power arises from meaning. It has to do with motive and it has to do with principle. Power is always associated with that which supports life itself. It appeals to the part of human nature that we call noble—in contrast to force, which we call crass. Power appeals to what uplifts, dignifies, and ennobles. Force must always be justified, whereas power requires no justification. Force is associated with the partial, power the whole. (p. 132)

David R. Hawkins
Power vs. Force

The Musician's Walk

*P*eople, especially artists, possess an innate fear of the analytical. They also seem to possess a fear of paradigm because it is direct contrast to the creative process or "living in the moment." In *The Musician's Soul* (GIA, 1999), I wrote about the fallacy of the phrase "living in the moment." By living in the moment, one gives permission to oneself to shut out the life lived or the life to be lived. Such a mindset can only inhibit one's humanness and ability to function as an artist in the world.

clearing away blockages

As stated in the first chapter of this book, paradigms are important. They provide an organized structure for thinking, understanding, and living. A good paradigm explains human behavior. The best paradigms provide a path for both correction and long-term improvement. I have found that it is easy to "identify" issues. One person I know constantly tells music students they have "blockages" that are inhibiting their music making. Blockages are bits of "life" that cause music to get "stopped up." The solution to those blockages? The most common response is, "That is your problem," or "Maybe you need therapy!"

90

Such a response is worse than the blockages themselves. Such advice approaches life issues from a position of *force* rather than a position of *power*. Moreover, such advice shows no compassion toward another human being. Force is always self-centered and manipulative. Power "blockages" are a fact of life; life is a series of blockages. It is easy to point the finger and accuse persons of "blockages," but what is the path to coping with these life barnacles? They cannot be avoided, and they cannot be removed once placed there by life. We need a paradigm for daily living and music making that will keep blockages in perspective and allow us to move ahead. We need a paradigm that heals rather than treats.

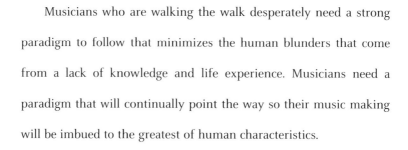

Musicians who are walking the walk desperately need a strong paradigm to follow that minimizes the human blunders that come from a lack of knowledge and life experience. Musicians need a paradigm that will continually point the way so their music making will be imbued to the greatest of human characteristics.

summary of the research

The work of Hawkins (2002), Diamond (1979), Weber (1982), Sheldrake (1981), and Land and Jarman (1992) puts forward a case for the valid study of consciousness through the mapping of energy fields. Maps of fields of human consciousness were developed through a methodology known as *attractor* research. Attractors are defined as an identifiable energy pattern that emerges from a seemingly unmeaningful mass of data. Attractors are magnetic fields emitted by individuals that can be measured spectrographically—or rather, holographically.

The research was conducted over a twenty-year period on thousands of subjects that represented a normal distribution of socio-economic classes, from normal psychological populations to abnormal populations. Subjects were examined in the United States, Mexico, South America, Northern Europe, and the Far East. The research design is based upon the science of kinesiology. Studies in kinesiology by Diamond identified a direct correlation between muscle strength and immediate weakness in that muscle ascribed to specific stimuli. Muscle tests were performed on subjects. Declarative statements correlating with words associated with states of human consciousness were read to the subjects. Muscle responses were charted with the use of a logarithmic scale. The design of the study is detailed in Diamond (*Behavioral Kinesiology*, 1979).

the paradigm

For those who have read *The Musician's Soul* and for those who have heard me speak, it is obvious that the paradigm of mimetics forms the core of how musicians should prepare their inner selves for music making. Mimetics compels one to understand the negative role that envy can play in destroying what is good in music.

Mimetics is a paradigm that must be in place before one embarks on the paradigm I will now present. It might do the reader well to revisit the chapter on mimetics in *The Musician's Soul.* If one is not mimetically "in the right place," then it will be difficult—if not impossible—for this next paradigm to point the way for the walk.

I stumbled upon the work of David Hawkins while researching this book; I believe his ideas can form the core of not only a philosophy for musicians but also a way of moving through life that always points us in the right direction. Hawkins uses the terms "power" and "force" in his discussions. Because of the negative connotations the word "force" engenders in musicians, I would like to use the word "core" as a synonym in these discussions. I would also suggest that at some point, every reader examine Hawkins' book, which is listed in the bibliography of this book.

Hawkins has identified levels of human consciousness, which he experimentally identified through energy fields. These specific energy fields exist in varying degrees in human beings. The lower energy fields exist in all of us; they seem to be a required part of the human condition. They are what I would consider "blockages." The lower energy fields can only be lessened and placed in perspective when higher energy fields are experienced. These energy fields are synonymous with human consciousness. Like mimetics, this, too, is a conscious act requiring our constant vigil to realize the greatest of human experiences: the walk that is not only in the right direction but that moves constantly upward as we live our lives through and with music. It is also important to note as I quote Dr. Hawkins' values that these values are logarithmic, not arithmetical. For example, 300 is not twice 150, but rather 10 to the 300th power. Hawkins points out that levels below 200 are "destructive in life in both the individual and society," and that all levels above 200 are constructive "expressions of power." The challenge for musicians is to strive for the upper levels of "power."

Hawkins has labeled the following human characteristics and has validated these levels through reliable, valid, qualitative research designs.

Chart of Kinesiology Energy Levels

20 . . . . shame
30 . . . . guilt
50 . . . . apathy
75 . . . . grief
100 . . . . fear
125 . . . . desire (envy)

```
150 . . . . . . . . . . . . . . . . . . . . . . anger
175 . . . . . . . . . . . . . . . . . . . . . . pride
200 . . . . . . . . . . . . . . . . . . . . . . courage
250 . . . . . . . . . . . . . . . . . . . . . . neutrality
310 . . . . . . . . . . . . . . . . . . . . . . willingness
350 . . . . . . . . . . . . . . . . . . . . . . acceptance
400 . . . . . . . . . . . . . . . . . . . . . . reason
500 . . . . . . . . . . . . . . . . . . . . . . LOVE
540 . . . . . . . . . . . . . . . . . . . . . . joy
600 . . . . . . . . . . . . . . . . . . . . . . peace
700–1000 . . . . . . . . . . . . . . . . . ENLIGHTENMENT
```

His paradigm is remarkable for many reasons, and highly applicable to musicians. Many musicians can experience success in the classroom and in the rehearsal room, and yet never move above the 400 level. The goal is to *know* and experience above the 400 level. However, I believe that without help and a total awareness, it is impossible to achieve that goal. In *The Musician's Soul*, mimetics provided a paradigm for moving musicians to the 500 level—LOVE. However, the issues addressed in *The Musician's Walk* have to do with musicians (1) never achieving love and care in their teaching and music making, and (2) because of a state of unawareness, consequently never moving into the 400 level and beyond.

Love is the key to the life walk of a musician. Without love, the walk is halting. We stumble from one musical experience to another. As Hawkins so eloquently points out, "As love becomes more and more unconditional, it begins to be experienced as inner joy. Joy arises from each moment of existence." He goes on to point out that

"from 540 up is the domain of saints, advanced spiritual students and healers. A capacity for enormous patience and persistence as a prolonged attitude in the face of prolonged adversity is characteristic of this energy field; the hallmark of this state is compassion." (p. 91)

He continues to point out a more remarkable truth. The achievement of level 600 and above is rare, but achievable. Achievable how? Through a constant awareness of people—a type of energy flow that feels as if it is in slow motion, but all is alive and radiant. *I believe great teachers and great musicians live in this place.* This level is achievable through constant awareness and sight of the goal of joy, peace, and enlightenment through the door of love. Simply stated, unless we are in a loving connection with all human beings with whom we work and make music, joy, peace, and enlightenment—or as Abraham Joshua Heschel states, "awe and wonder"—are impossible. Music becomes a lifeless vessel, which carries sound without meaning. *Music is capable of being everything or nothing,* depending on the transmitter and the teacher. Music can exist as sound without meaning. Unfortunately, it does exist in this form in many classrooms and ensembles. Core (or "power," as Hawkins calls it) can only be achieved by entering, at the very least, into the 400 level. At the 400 level and above, these are high-energy patterns, veritable human vortexes of energy that clarify the walk and give it both purpose and direction.

core and force pairs to heighten consciousness: the negative effect of "crazymakers"

Hawkins has come up with a remarkable list of adjectives that make up what he calls "the fabric of life." He believes, as do I, that simple but daily reflection on these contrasting pairs can raise the consciousness of a musician and, thus, create a new state of awareness from which music achieves new depth and understanding. Music teaching and learning using this new awareness moves mundane teaching from pedantic to truly inspired. It is all a question of awareness of the walk. On the left are powerful (or core) patterns, which all calibrate at the 200 levels or above according to Hawkins; on the right are weak, negative (or energy) patterns that create negative force rather than positive core.

Note that there is a fine line of meaning between the pairings of the terms in the list below. If meanings of the terms are unclear, consult the Oxford Dictionary for clarification.

Core Positive Energies (above 400)	Force Negative Energies (below 400)
abundant	excessive
accepting	rejecting
allowing	controlling
appreciative	envious
agreeable	condescending
authoritative	dogmatic
aware	preoccupied
being	having
believing	insisting
brilliant	clever
candid	calculating
charitable	prodigal
concerned	judgmental
conciliatory	inflexible
confident	arrogant
confronting	harassing
conscious	unaware
considerate	indulgent
determined	stubborn
devoted	possessive
doing	getting
educating	persuading
energetic	agitated
enlivening	exhausting
ethical	equivocal
fair	scrupulous
forgiving	resenting
grateful	indebted
healing	irritating
honest	legal
humble	diffident
inspired	mundane

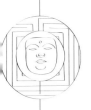

Core Positive Energies (above 400)	Force Negative Energies (below 400)
inviting	urging
involved	obsessed
kind	cruel
leading	coercive
noble	pompous
nurturing	draining
observant	suspicious
patient	avid
peaceful	belligerent
powerful	forceful
principled	expedient
receiving	grasping
respectful	demeaning
serene	dull
sharing	hoarding
spontaneous	impulsive
valuing	exploitive
virtuous	celebrated

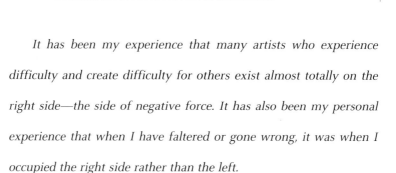

It has been my experience that many artists who experience difficulty and create difficulty for others exist almost totally on the right side—the side of negative force. It has also been my personal experience that when I have faltered or gone wrong, it was when I occupied the right side rather than the left.

If we continue to love ourselves and others, the way to the left will be found. That is our salvation in this art. It is possible to walk one's entire walk on that right side. The lower energy levels of fear, desire, anger, and pride seem to be empathetic with those who couple them with the highly negative force of one's ego. Without the overpowering force of ego, such people are powerless. But combined with ego, such an existence leads to relationships and music making that is tortured, dishonest, and illusionary at best. Unfortunately, it is possible to be a musician living in these places, and many do, often achieving notoriety living in such a place. These persons are usually persons endowed with tremendous musical gifts, tremendous egos, and little human compassion, care, or love for others. By sheer force, they inflict music onto others.

But great teachers and musicians do not live in such a place. They consistently strive to understand the subtle semantic differences between the terms on the right and the terms on the left side of the list. Constant reflection that breeds awareness is the key. In the list above, I have chosen those pairs that I think illustrate the issues that confront us on the musician's walk. (For a complete list, consult Hawkins (pp. 146–148).) Reflection over and over again on these word pairings can provide the vehicle or paradigm for the best "energy levels" for the musician's walk.

If this paradigm is to work, both terms must be considered concurrently and daily for meaning to be derived from their semantic relationship. I would also like to point out that musicians who thrive on hurting others to build up their own ego centers exist exclusively in the right column. Further, those persons tend to live their lives exclusively *below* the 400 level on the Chart of Kinesiology Energy Levels (shown on page 93). It is possible to exist for one's entire life below this level, and many do. However, they can be best typified as Julia Cameron has labeled such persons in her books—as "crazymakers." Crazymakers create mimetic storms and conflict wherever they are, and either justify the havoc they heap on others as "artistic behavior" or scapegoat such behavior as justified for their "art." In other words, inhumane behavior toward others is justified because they are gifted artists. Such mental attitudes insulate such persons from the feelings and human connection to other people. They never realize such a connection because they become so insulated and so numb that it affects their ability to hear profoundly and honestly. They, consequently, never hear their own music: the sound is unable to teach them anything about life, and the composer's voice is hopelessly sublimated because of their avoidance of human issues and the overall human condition at the time.

It is also interesting to note that such persons live constantly somewhere between the energy levels of 125 and 200. They tend to anger easily with others, and they have intense pride about their music making and opinions. Such people do not realize that their low

 energy level, which is not counterbalanced by the

higher energy levels, represses all those who naively make music with them. They continually live at the 200 level to inflict their feelings on others, while being closed to accepting *ideas* or even *love* from others. These crazymakers sabotage not only their own creative process but also the creative process of all others around them.

125 . . . . desire (envy)
150 . . . . anger
175 . . . . pride
200 . . . . courage

It may be helpful to further define these terms and their impact upon human behavior. Hawkins (2002) defines these terms at length. I present short summaries to begin the clarification process.

Desire. In *The Musician's Soul,* I spent a great deal of time defining *envy,* which is a synonym for desire. Envy determines much of our life course and certainly has a detrimental effect on musicians. Envy becomes an addiction and is more important than life itself. Persons consumed in envy are usually unaware that they are envious, and such low energy forces tend to repel others.

Anger. It is important to know that anger can lead to either constructive or destructive action, according to Hawkins. Anger can

102

move one toward freedom. Anger can also move one toward resentment and revenge.

Pride. Pride is totally dependent on external conditions. While pride in good accomplishments is desirable, most often pride is a label for both arrogance and denial. Negative pride is used as a justification for cruel and inhumane treatment of other artists.

Courage. Persons who dwell within the negative aspects of desire, anger, and pride can seldom rise to the level of *true* courage. An overwhelming combination of the energies of desire, anger, and pride can create a false sense that feels like pride. Instead of being true pride, the feeling is a justification of desire and anger. True courage is exciting, challenging, stimulating, and truly radiant. If one can understand the qualities of courage, then real productivity and creativity begin and thrive.

the antidote for crazymakers

The best antidote to those negative energies is to live in the left column—the positive energies. The left column also constitutes a framework for ethical guidelines for musicians, designed to bring about and achieve a shift in awareness.

How does one live on the left side of the list? Remember that the words are semantic representations of human states.

1. Define each term in your own consciousness and quantify that meaning with life experience.

2. Consult the list every day and ponder its meaning. In essence, a short period of meditation on portions of the list (or even specific pairings) should be part of the daily ritual.

3. Keep a daily journal where you can put into words what the pairings mean. Search for inspirational quotes that help to define the core energies. Most importantly, it is centrally important to clearly define all of the terms in the left column for yourself and your life.

If this "ritual" is maintained daily, the left column will become a way of life. For musicians, it will transform itself into a living, breathing philosophy of music teaching and music making.

It is helpful to keep the following statements in mind as "inspiration." Just as mimetics (as detailed in *The Musician's Soul*) is important for shoring up our way of being with and teaching others, the development and strengthening of the core energies is the most important thing an artist can do to ensure his/her own artistic development and growth. Remember that the rules of mimetics are a prerequisite to acquisition of these core energies: The conscious decision to love and care for self and others opens the door to a higher, more brilliant way of living and art that *is* the core energies.

104

Such spiritual work, like other intensive pursuits—can be arduous and frequently requires the development of specific tools for the task, including an extremely focused intent and unfailing concentration. The difficulty of inner work results from the great effort required to escape from the familiar gravity of lower attractor fields and move to the influence of a higher field. (p. 263)

The agency of change in spiritual struggles of personal metamorphosis is always beyond the power of the seeker. Great Saints, such as Francis of Assisi, have typically asserted that they were the channels of a higher power—they've taken no credit for personal initiative in achieving their state, which they attributed to Grace. This is illustrative of the instrumentation where the newcomer from a lesser level of awareness is transformed "by osmosis." (p. 267)

David R. Hawkins

Power vs. Force

"The sounds of music calm our volatile souls."

"Road to Tuzigoot"

Chapter 11

Musicians Heal Yourselves: Listening in a New Way

When you first become aware of harmonics as a phenomenon of sound, your entire way of listening becomes altered. You may hear harmonics in the dripping of a tap or overtones in the wind as it rushes past your window. As you become aware of harmonics, your listening patterns change and, as this occurs, so does your consciousness. (p. 74)

Listening is an active activity, as opposed to hearing which may be understood as passive activity. Listening involves really using our ears as an organ of consciousness. When we hear, we do not discriminate between the sounds around us. We may be unaware of them. (p. 81)

Jonathan Goldman
Healing Sounds

Emotion, because it brings feelings and connects you to feeling, allows you to recognize different states of consciousness. The logical mind does not allow you to recognize states of consciousness because it holds onto its own identity. It is locked into the boundary of ego and does not want to recognize other areas. Feeling, however, always acknowledges other areas because feeling discerns the difference. You can read the signs and definitions by the energy that you call feeling. It is, in actuality, a vibration. Sound brings about states of emotional feeling. When you create harmonics of sound, it reminds your body of something. As you allow your sound to play your body, you discover a frequency that you have sought. (p. 130)

Renee Brodie

Heal Yourself with Sound and Color

It is possible to record the waves produced by singing bowls. It was found that among the wave patterns of different singing bowls, there is a measurable wave pattern which is equivalent to the alpha waves produced by the brain. These bowls, in particular, instill a sense of deep relaxation and inner space opening up. (p. 42)

Eva Rudy Jansen

Singing Bowls

The challenge in developing vibratory awareness is to allow perception to be free, not bound by our enthusiasm to find out what will happen. (p. 23)

Don G. Campbell

The Roar of Silence

The Musician's Walk

*G*iven the materials presented in the last chapter, allow me to step into a likely unfamiliar area and present some theories for you to consider. This material came about after a series of serendipitous events that were impossible to ignore.

First, let me begin by making several subjective observations about musicians. I have no objective research to support these points, just twenty-five years of observation of choral singers and a newfound observation of my own life.

1. Musicians and artists tend to be somewhat emotionally and spiritually volatile.

2. Musicians experience extremes of emotional highs and lows.

3. In periods of extreme volatility, musicians tend to vent or scapegoat either those around them or the ensembles with whom they work.

4. Musicians remain in agitated states until they have contact with music.

5. Musicians are able to hear more in the world that surrounds them than others can.

6. Musicians are seldom in an agitated or volatile state while music is being sounded.

7.   Musicians in agitated or volatile states are seldom calmed through conversation or calming words.

8.   Left in a volatile state, musicians seldom make logical or rational decisions about any subject.

9.   Most musicians do not use music or sound as a part of their emotional repair process.

If we look back at our lives in music, each of us probably became involved in music because we felt "better" when we either heard music or made music. It was, in part, the calming, healing, and reassuring quality of music that probably drew most—if not all—of us to music. If asked why we are musicians, we would probably give such replies as "I Love the beauty of the music," or "I love the color of the sounds," or "I love how music makes me feel." All of these statements have a certain kind of subjective validity that probably resonances with each of us. But if we examine the seminal events in our lives, music probably restored emotional order in a way that nothing else in life could.

For me, there are some seminal events that drew me unknowingly to music.

The   Musician's   Walk

bach   and   the   boy   scouts

I must have been only ten or eleven years of age and was going to my weekly Boy Scout meeting held at the UCC Church in town. The church had recently completed the building of a new sanctuary and installation of a new organ. The sanctuary was being dedicated within this particular week.

For some reason, I was very early for the scout meeting that night. As I approached the door to the social hall of the church, I noticed the plastic that had sealed the entrance door to the new sanctuary had been removed! So I snuck into the new church on my hands and knees to take a peek. As I crawled into the church, the most amazing sound I had ever heard began to surround me. I can still "hear" that sound. It was Bach, and from what I remember, it may have been *Prelude and Fugue in E-Flat* on "St. Anne." I remember being somewhat overcome by the sound. All I wanted to do was to lie down and hide beneath a pew and listen. So lie down I did—and I missed part of the meeting. I remember looking at my watch after a period of time and realizing that almost forty-five minutes had passed.

I now still remember that calm and the beauty I experienced as a boy that day. I have never forgotten the feeling it created in me. I believe this was one of the pivotal events that turned me toward music.

a s t a r i u s

I take time each year to travel to Sedona, Arizona. For those who have been there, you will understand why I go. For those who have never been there, you are missing one of the great experiences of life.

One of the activities of tourists and locals is to observe the spectacular desert sunset. There are many locations from which to observe a sunset in Sedona, but the best one is just below the airport entrance. It is on a bluff at one of the highest points within the town limits of Sedona. Each evening in the summer, there may be several hundred people gathered there at the appointed hour. There are also local Indians selling wares, and at times, there may be others there offering spiritual "new age" services for a fee.

Now understand, I had been going to Sedona for approximately ten years and thought I had seen everything and knew everything. But one evening, I encountered something I knew nothing about.

As I arrived at the bluff, there was a man playing a didgeridoo, an instrument of the Australian Aboriginals, which is made of some part of a tree, that is the Australian equivalent to the Swiss Alpine horn.

The man who was playing called himself Astarius. He had a small sign next to him and a cassette bag of his own recordings, which he was selling. I had heard didgeridoo music before, but I must say I never heard that music with such range and expressivity. Moreover, Astarius could play for long lengths of time because of an amazing circular breathing technique. So I started to peruse his recordings and purchased a few (listed in the bibliography of this book). Astarius stopped playing to take my money and said he would like to give me a "sound healing." He told me he was a Reiki Master and he would give me an experience that "I would never forget."

"Sure," I thought to myself. "That's right. I am going to have a life-changing experience in front of hundreds of people." Not wanting to sit in front of the people with a didgeridoo pointed at my head, I volunteered my fellow traveler, Eric, who was standing nearby. I said, "Do it to him." Thank goodness, Eric agreed. So I watched. And I became immediately amazed and pulled in by the sound.

After Eric was done (he served well in his guinea pig capacity), I asked Astarius to "do it to me." He was kind and said it would be his honor. He asked my name. I said, "James." He said, "My name is Astarius. Close your eyes, breathe deeply, and allow the sound to do its work." (See www.astarius.com.) For ten minutes, Astarius sounded the didgeridoo. My body vibrated and empathetically resonated with a feeling that went beyond any massage treatment I had ever experienced! When he was done, I felt physically relaxed, and *very* grounded, centered, and calmed. I was amazed. I was deeply changed

114 and transformed. As evidence, I present a picture of the author being

"didgeridooed"!

c r y s t a l   b o w l   r e d i s c o v e r y

The next day I happened into Crystal Magic, a store in Sedona. As I browsed around the store, I noticed a section of quartz crystal singing bowls; I had never seen so many in one place. (I must confess that the sound these bowls produce has always had a profound effect on me.) I asked the owner to give me a lesson in playing the bowls. He took a wooden wand and began to set every bowl on the shelves (about six) in vibration. The sound was amazing; again I felt the same as the previous evening of "didgeridoo therapy." How did I feel? Immediately upon hearing the sound, I felt very grounded, open, calm, peaceful and, at the same time, vibrant. In thinking about these experiences, I am convinced this is an avenue that may help many

musicians access the "right place" from which to make music.

background and history of the quartz crystal bowl

Many cultures recognize the importance of music and sound as a healing tool. In ancient India, Asia, Africa, Europe, and among the Aborigines and American Indians, the practice of using sound to heal and achieve balance has existed for centuries. The Tibetans still use bells, chimes, bowls, and chanting as the foundation of their spiritual practice. In Bali, the gong and drum are used in ceremonies to uplift and to send messages. The Australian Aboriginals and Native American shamans use vocal toning and repetitive sounds, along with instruments created from nature, in sacred ceremony to adjust any imbalance of the spirit, emotions, or physical being. The priests of ancient Egypt knew how to use vowel sounds to resonate their energy centers, or chakras.

There is a direct link between different parts of the body and specific sounds. Such a technique appears extremely old, yet healing through sound goes back even further, at least as far back as Atlantis, where the power of sound was combined with the power of crystal. In fact, some people today still refer to the crystal singing bowls as being Atlantean crystal bowls.

116

At the present time, the Native American Hopi prophecy is being fulfilled with the "Coming of the Rainbow People," through the keepers of the crystal bowls. This ancient wisdom has emerged to heal and uplift the consciousness of the universe through pure crystal tone. Edgar Cayce, the American psychic, and Rudolf Steiner, German philosopher, educator, and artistic genius, both predicted that "pure tones will be used for healing before the end of this century."

It is thought and believed by many who practice sound therapies that everything in the universe is in a state of vibration, and each object or person has a resonant frequency that is their optimal vibration. The chakras, bones, and organs in the body all possess a different resonant frequency. When an organ (or other part of the body) is vibrating out of tune or nonharmoniously, it is called "disease." A body is in a healthy state of being when each cell and each organ create a resonance that is in harmony with the whole being. Vibrational therapy is based on the idea that all illness or disease is characterized by blockage in the channels on some level, such as in acupuncture meridians, arteries, veins, nerves, and chakras (energy centers). When there is a blockage, the organ in question stops vibrating at a healthy frequency and, thus, results in some kind of illness. Using sound and light, one can break up, dissolve, and remove those blockages that initiate in our light or etheric body. Ultrasound (very high-frequency sound), well known as a diagnostic tool for fetal development, is also being used to cleanse clogged arteries and break up kidney stones.

The body may be seen as a pattern of visible frequencies that produces an auric color field. The aura changes as it reflects emotional states of consciousness and, thus, the physiological status. The appearance of the aura is also conditioned by the qualities and activity of each chakra. A chakra may be underactive, overactive, or blocked. These may be temporary conditions or reflect a more deeply held pattern. For example, sudden emotional stress may drive the solar plexus into overactive churning, whereas long-term emotional stress may cause a person to nearly shut down the solar plexus chakra so the person may avoid feeling any more hurt. Of course, this also means the person lessens the ability to feel at all, including pleasure.

The sounds of the crystal bowls are thought to help balance the chakras in two ways. At the same time as the disharmonious conditions are being adjusted or removed, a sacred space is created for strengthening of the person's Higher Self connection or "Divine Blueprint." When an unbalanced energetic condition is removed, it is always wise to fill the void created with the highest aspect of source the person is willing to embrace. The sound waves from the crystal bowls emit a pure, holographic template of radiant sound that builds a "Jacob's ladder" to the Divine.

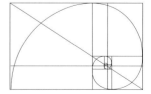

118

The pure tones of the crystal bowls produce a vibrational sound field that resonates the light body energy centers (chakras) and corresponding physical areas. There are seven musical notes that correspond to the seven colors of the rainbow, and these are related to the seven main chakras which, in turn, correspond to different areas of the endocrine gland system. A series of pure crystal tone sessions facilitates the rebalancing of each receiver back into an elevated level of etheric radiance. The effects are enhanced because the bowls are made of quartz. Silicon crystal acts as an oscillator, magnifying and transmitting pure tone. This is why pure quartz crystal is used in the most advanced telecommunications systems. Like a powerful radio transmitter, the crystal bowls transmit energy into the atmosphere, filling a person's hearing with vibrational radiance that translates into the seven main colors of the rainbow.

As the pure crystal tones affect brain wave activity, one can travel into an altered state of consciousness. As different parts of the brain are affected, it is probable that different hormones and neuro-chemicals are released that suppress pain, overcome addictions, strengthen willpower, and foster creativity. Each crystal bowl is made of almost 100 percent silicon quartz (sometimes there are small amounts of other natural minerals that were found with the quartz). One reason why the pure tones vibrate our bodies is that our bodies have a natural affinity to quartz. The human body is composed of many crystalline substances: The bones, blood, and DNA are crystalline in structure, as well as the liquid crystal-colloidal structure of the brain. Even on a molecular level, our cells contain silica, which balances our electromagnetic energies.

Quartz crystal music holds the vibration of white light, which ultimately refracts into the rainbow and acts directly on our chakras when played. It has the power to bring about a positive shift in our consciousness, and as our awareness expands, we grow close to our original selves and start to reflect the highest radiance in our physical form. Physicists know that quartz is able to maintain the balance of electromagnetic energies between its north and south poles, enabling it to play a key role in timekeeping systems. The same electromagnetic field exists within all life forms. Quartz balances our own electromagnetic energies.

Quartz crystal, as a holographic light template, is able to hold, transmit, and receive thought forms. In *Healing Sounds: The Power of Harmonics* (2002), Jonathan Goldman writes, "The intention behind the sound is of extreme importance. It may, in fact, be as important as the actual sounds that are created." The power of thought is the means by which we create our reality. Nothing can be created unless it is first thought. When using crystal to rebalance, the crystal amplifies the thought programmed within it. The crystal has

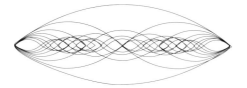

120

this amazing property and, thus, can be used to bring out a special feeling or quality in people and simultaneously release and replace thought forms that are not of the highest radiance for the listener.

musicians and the quartz crystal bowls

In my previous books, I have encouraged musicians to use various devices, from rattles to Swiss exercise balls, to help them in their musical work. While on the surface they may appear "gimmicky," those who have used them have likely found that they are valuable tools to open the door for musicians to experiences that will deepen and enhance their understanding of the music-making process. I have begun to use and explore the use of the quartz crystal bowls in my conducting classes, ensembles, and conducting coaching.

Why do the quartz crystal bowls work? Honestly, I do not know of any objective research. However, I do know they have produced profound changes in me and many of my students, and I do have some theories as to why they have such effects upon musicians.

First, I made a case in *The Musician's Soul* as to how important it is for musicians to spend time with themselves—to be able to access quiet and calm for music to speak through us. I have suggested meditation, mimetics, and other "devices" to access this calm place. Through this new type of sound "therapy," I have come to realize one important factor about us as musicians and teachers.

As I have noted in my earlier books, many things in the world cause us to "close." Closure in musicians or in anyone else is a given part of the life experience. The challenge becomes whether or not to struggle to find ways of opening ourselves so that, ultimately, we can hear in a new and profound way.

If you observe your patterns of behavior, I am sure you will see that most likely sound—and only sound—can cause you to calm and open. Meditation and quiet may help, but music is the ultimate spiritual "salve." When we are making music, I am never angry, spiteful, jealous, ego centered, or questioning as the music is being sounded. For the most part, I am always calm, peaceful, happy, open and, of recent years, caring and loving. But when the music stops, the influences of the world around me eat at my spirit and cause me to think things I wish I wouldn't.

You see, I believe we all are musicians for one important reason. The *sounds* of music calm our volatile souls and give meaning to our lives and the lives of people who come into contact with our music making. That being said, we can't have an ensemble follow us around and help us throughout our day. However, we could use the sound of the quartz crystal bowls to re-channel ourselves to a "good" place.

122 Think of it this way. If you have never heard the sound of a quartz crystal bowl, depending on the size of the bowl, the sound overtakes your being. You feel a vibration throughout you that seems to have an incredibly calming effect as long as your eyes are closed and you concentrate on your breathing. In fact, on some days, you will even see colors. Not only does the bowl help me, but unknowingly, I come away hearing differently. I hear more deeply, and I hear more "things" in sound, their overtones and the subtle complexities that make up the sound.

Recently, we added hand-held singing bowls, or quartz "chakra" bowls, to the opening of our Evening of Readings and Carols program at Westminster. At the end of an arrangement of "I Wonder As I Wander," a short vocal improvisation was inserted, as well as the playing of four of these bowls. At the end of the improvisation, only the sounding of the bowls remained. The entire room became silent when the sound of the bowls became apparent. It was an amazing experience to behold.

This book talks about an ethical code for musicians. The main reason for this code is that when music is absent, when sound is absent, musicians may behave toward others in many undesirable ways. When sound is not present, musicians are "in trouble" in terms of relationships with people around them. In addition to understanding "how" we should behave, we must also equip ourselves

to use sound in a rejuvenative way. By listening to these bowls with their almost unending tones, the sound causes one to find center. The constancy of the sound brings both calm and a new awareness that was not present before the sound of the bowls was present. I have found that these marvelous crystal bowls can become your best friend, causing you to access and rediscover your calm center out of which all other life decisions are made.

further reading on this subject

Brodie, Renee. *The Healing Tones of Crystal Bowls.* Vancouver, Canada: Aroma Art Limited, 1996.

Campbell, Don G. *The Roar of Silence: Healing Powers of Breath, Tone and Music.* Wheaton, IL: Theosophical Publishing House, 1989.

Goldman, Jonathan. *Healing Sounds: The Power of Harmonics.* Rochester, VT: Healing Arts Press, 2002.

Thondup, Tulku. *The Healing Power of the Mind.* Boston, MA: Shambhala, 1998.

Section Two

Journeying In

"...the ability to give without undue thought of gain..."

"Enlightened Sphere"

Chapter 12

Understanding Why Artists Hurt Others

So Socrates was mistaken: it's not the unexamined life that is not worth living; it's the uncommitted life. There is no smaller package in the world than that of a person all wrapped up in himself. Love is our business. (p. 12)

William Sloane Coffin

The Heart Is a Little to the Left

The opposite of humanity is brutality, the failure to acknowledge the humanity of one's fellow man, the failure to be sensitive to his needs, to his situation. Brutality is often due to a failure of imagination as well as the tendency to treat a person as a generality, to regard a person as an average man. (p. 47)

There are two primary ways in which man relates himself to the world that surrounds him: manipulation and appreciation. In the first way he sees in what surrounds him things to be handled, forces to be

128

managed, objects to be put to use. In the second way he sees in what surrounds him things to be acknowledged, understood, valued or admired. (p. 82)

Abraham Joshua Heschel
Who Is Man?

Jealousy and envy revolve around comparing oneself to others and judging them. At an extreme, this becomes resentment of the accomplishments of others and a paranoid fear that others will outdo one. This judgmental attitude breeds condescension and a flurry of activity around setting things right—that is, in accord with one's own view of how things should be—and so imposing one's order. (p. 313)

Tara Bennett-Goleman
Emotional Alchemy

Temporary insanity may take the form of a dark mood, which may come over you, making you feel testy, angry, or depressed. This is usually not a long, black depression, but rather a deep-blue moodiness that is a challenge to the people near you. In those minutes, hours, or days, you are not present in the usual way. When people approach you, they run up against your mood and may not be able to penetrate it. (p. 263)

Thomas Moore
Dark Nights of the Soul

To Love

Is to discover and complete one's self

In someone other than oneself.

An act impossible of general realization on Earth

So long as each can see in the neighbor no more than

A closed fragment following its own course

Through the world.

It is precisely

This state of isolation that will end

If we begin to discover in each other

Not merely the elements of one and the same thing,

But of a single spirit in search of itself.

The existence of such a power

Becomes possible in the curvature of a world

Capable of neogenesis.

Teilhard de Chardin
Meditation

Why should I wish to see God better than this day?

I see something of God each hour of the twenty-four, and each moment then; In the faces of men and women I see God, and in my own face in the glass; I see letters from God dropt [*sic*] in the street— and every one is sign'd [*sic*] by God's name.

Walt Whitman

When someone whom I have helped or in whom I have placed great hope harms me with great injustice, may I see that one as a sacred friend. (p. 102)

Tenzin Gyatso, The Fourteenth Dalai Lama
"Eight Verses for Training the Mind"
The Compassionate Life

When somebody insults you, you have to become a receiver; you have to accept what he says, only then can you react. But if you don't accept, if you simply remain detached, if you keep the distance, if you remain cool, what can he do? (p. 133)

Osho

Awareness

Why, for so many years, were conductors so oblivious to the corruption of their snap judgments? Because we are often careless with our powers of rapid cognition. We don't know where our first impressions come from or precisely what they mean, so we don't always appreciate their fragility. Taking our powers of rapid cognition seriously means we have to acknowledge the subtle influences that can alter or undermine or bias the products of our unconscious. Judging music sounds like the simplest of tasks. It is not.

Too often we are resigned to what happens in the blink of an eye. It doesn't seem like we have much control over whatever bubbles to the surface from our unconscious. But we do, and if we can control the

131

environment in which rapid cognition takes place, then we can control rapid cognition. (pp. 252–253)

When it comes to the task of understanding ourselves and our world, I think we pay too much attention to those grand themes and too little to the particulars of those fleeting moments. But what would happen if we took our instincts seriously? What if we stopped scanning the horizon with our binoculars and began instead examining our own decision making and behavior through the most powerful of microscopes?

...the task of making sense of ourselves and our behavior requires that we acknowledge there can be as much value in the blink of an eye as in months of rational analysis. (pp. 16–17)

Malcolm Gladwell

Blink

While the development of the ego gives the unfolding person certain essential powers of discrimination and strengths of self-definition that the child's mind does not have, there is an inherent danger—that the evolving personality should identify itself completely with it and define the whole range of its possibilities within its narrow terms.

Also, very few, if any, of us develop entirely healthy egos; mostly, our ego development is conditioned by parental, social, and religious restrictions. Many of us also will be marked at an early age by various forms of trauma—whether abuse or abandonment or other forms of

132

psychological difficulty. In some cases this experience of trauma will be so severe that any further unfolding of the personality will be aborted; in most cases, wounds will be inflicted on the psyche around which defenses will be built like hardened scars. (p. 49)

Andrew Harvey

The Direct Path

The longest, most arduous trip in the world is often the journey from the head to the heart. Until that round trip is completed, we remain at war with ourselves. And, of course, those at war with themselves are apt to make casualties of others, including friends and loved ones. (p. 126)

William Sloane Coffin

Credo

*I*n his book, *Changing Minds*, Howard Gardner makes the point that the phenomenon of changing one's mind is the least understood of familiar human experiences. And he talks of not just changing one's mind but of bringing about significant changes in one's mind. For those of you familiar with Gardner's work, he has codified six or seven identifiable intelligences in human beings. But he also writes about another group of intelligences: *interpersonal* intelligence and *intrapersonal* intelligence. Interpersonal intelligence is used to discriminate among people and figure out their motivations, work with them and, if necessary, as Gardner puts it, "manipulate" them. It seems as if musicians at times lack interpersonal skills—that is, the ability to figure out people's motivations and why they do things.

The subject of this chapter is a difficult one to discuss, but its major premise must be brought forward for thought and reflection. It seems to be a common thread that many artists, when faced with either life or musical frustrations, lash out at people around them in the most hurtful of ways. It is almost as if all of the highly developed sensitivities they use in creating art are tossed to the wayside to defend or enhance their own personal ego.

I still believe that mimetics is key to avoiding such situations. But there are times when life and musical events thrust us into the center of such storms. We lose any interpersonal intelligence we may have acquired to help us through the moment and resort instead to imposing our will upon others, no matter how hurtful. Most often, "the music" is used as a scrim, shield, or justification for actions that are, simply put, inhumane.

Rules, reminders, and ways of doing things form the foundation for avoiding such behaviors. If one spends a great deal of time defining an ethical code that clearly identifies pathways for change (i.e., a vision for interaction and behavior that has as its foundation a

134

profound sense of compassion and love), then highly volatile situations can be either diffused or avoided.

For those who lash out, the best antidote is perhaps silence, or at least quiet speaking. William Sloane Coffin has said that when preaching, always deliver difficult messages in quiet tones. It may also be necessary in these moments to think well of oneself in the middle of such an onslaught and to silently offer love and care to the person on the attack.

Music—and art in general—teaches many things. What it teaches best is vulnerability. Musicians lack the ability to function while in a vulnerable state. When one is vulnerable, one is hurt easier. Many musicians subconsciously know when others are most vulnerable, and they choose those times to say and do things that can augur injury. Every artist must acknowledge that the possibility to do this is real and take steps to acquire a newfound awareness about the possibility of doing this. They must also take preemptive steps to avoid such actions at all costs.

The price for not doing this is steep. The music will suffer. The music and art always suffer. We almost never return after such incidents to the state of vulnerability that was present before the lashing out, giving up a bit of ourselves with each incident until reaching a point where there is little love or good left in our actions. We could view it as spending our "human" capital. Such capital, once spent, can almost never be replaced. Such capital is always spent in moments of unawareness.

So perhaps it is unawareness of the world and one's place in the world that breeds such inhumanity from artists. That is also to say that if we work to maintain total awareness throughout our music making and our lives, such incidents will never occur. I do not think it is an exaggeration to state that it is unaware persons who hurt others—and who are unaware that they have done so. They do so almost in a trance-like, distant state. Unawareness can provide a distinct protection for the ego. William Sloane Coffin calls it being all wrapped up in oneself. Buber talks of being aware of only the "I" and never the "thou." Buddha talks of an absence of compassion. Thomas Moore states this dilemma and its symptoms in more direct terms.

In therapy I have encountered people who were deeply disturbed and covered it over with their brilliance. What I saw in them was not irony at all, but a gulf between their emotions and their way of life. They didn't convert their conflicts into creativity but instead created a shield of aloof superiority that thinly covered the inferiority occasioned by their inner torment. Interestingly, their creative work fell short of the brilliance they feigned, as though it was necessary to reconcile with the pain in order to fire the imagination. (p. 111)

Thomas Moore
_____
Dark Nights of the Soul

136   In his book, *Changing Minds*, Howard Gardner believes that minds *can* be changed. This change can come from without; that is, one's inhumanity causes such turmoil that one's music and career suffer. Jolted into a new awareness, one changes. Or one can make a preemptive change of mind by operating under a code that is born out of deep thought and reflection. Hence, the ultimate direction of this book is toward a self-constructed code of ethics. That code of ethics must always be governed by an acute sense of self, self worth, and awarenesses.

Another way to consider this is that the musician's walk must be done in a state of profound and glorious awareness of the world and persons around the musician. Just  as the labyrinth causes one to change direction as one moves toward the center, so, too, may one have to change course a bit in one's life so music making can remain likewise glorious and luminescent. Ironically, Fred Rogers perhaps says it best in a recent book issued posthumously by his wife:

Love isn't a state of perfect caring. It is an active noun like struggle. To love someone is to strive to accept that person exactly the way he or she is, right here and now. (p. 53)

Mutually caring relationships require kindness and patience, tolerance, optimism, joy in the other's achievements, confidence in oneself, and the ability to give without undue thought of gain. We need to accept the fact that it's not in the power of any human being to provide all these things all the time. For any of us, mutually caring relationships will also include some measure of unkindness and impatience, intolerance, pessimism, envy, self-doubt, and disappointment. (p. 78)

When we love a person, we accept him or her exactly as is: the lovely with the unlovely, the strong along with the fearful, the true mixed in with the façade, and of course, the only way we can do it is by accepting ourselves that way. (p. 95)

Fred Rogers

The World According to Mister Rogers

"Music accurately reflects the human ingredients used in its formulation

"Offerings

Chapter 13

The "Real" Sound of Music

In every artist's development the germ of the latter work is always found in the earlier. The nucleus around which the artist's intellect builds his work is himself...and this changes little from birth to death.

The only real influence I've ever had was myself. (p. xii)

Edward Hopper

The Soul's Code by James Hillman

No man can know where he is going unless he knows exactly where he has been and exactly how he arrived at his present place. (p. 68)

Maya Angelou

Walking in This World by Julia Cameron

140

As artists, we are spiritual sharks. The ruthless truth is that if we don't keep moving, we sink to the bottom and die. The choice is very simple: we can insist on resting on our laurels, or we can begin anew. The stringent requirement of a sustained creative life is the humility to start again, to begin anew. (p. 93)

Many of us have made a virtue out of deprivation. We have embraced a long-suffering artistic anorexia as a martyr's cross. We have used it to feed a false sense of spirituality grounded in being good, meaning superior. This seductive, faux spirituality is the Virtue Trap. Spirituality has often been misused as a route to an unloving solitude, a stance where we proclaim ourselves above our human nature. This spiritual superiority is really only one more form of denial. (p. 37)

Often we involve ourselves with crazymakers in order to be creative ourselves. Crazymakers are those personalities that create storm centers. They are often charismatic, frequently charming, highly inventive, and powerfully persuasive. And for the creative person in their vicinity, they are enormously destructive. If you are involved with a crazymaker, it is very important that you admit that fact. Admit that you are being used—and admit that you are using them to sabotage your own trajectory. As much as you are being exploited by your crazymaker, you, too, are using that person to block your creative flow. (p. 13)

Julia Cameron
Inspirations

$\mathcal{M}$usic is capable of acquiring many disguises. In fact, recognizing inspired music that truly reflects human characteristics can be elusive if one is not careful. One can be mislead with the wonder of technical achievement: impeccable pitch, dynamic rhythm, and compelling musical line. Listening in an outward kind of way has the ability within one's own normal illusion, as the psychologists call it, to be fascinated with the surface shimmer but never really aurally dive beneath the surface. Allow me to speak from the perspective of a conductor, since that is the one I know best. Feel free to apply the paradigm to the musical situation in which you live your musical life.

What makes a truly profound performance? Certainly all the "benchmarks" of a good performance can be heard: great pitch, an exciting and vital musical sense, a viewpoint on interpretation, and even a viewpoint on the part of the conductor and the ensemble about the piece's relationship to the human experience in some way. Music can be disguised to sound great to a vast majority of listeners. But what marks that form of musical expression which can touch audiences in such profound ways as to change their very lives within the complexities of their day-to-day world?

I once heard a conductor remark after coming off of a series of concerts that the music making was "special" and profound. I found that difficult to comprehend because this person in his day-to-day

142 routine practiced relationships with others that bordered on hateful at worst, and demeaning and degrading at best. Do such persons really believe they are trustees of the human intent of great composers? Yes, the performances were "beautiful." But the beauty is different. For me, it is like looking at a reproduction of a great work of art. If one looks at a Giclee print reproduction of a piece, the colors and shapes are exact. From a distance, it might be hard to tell the original from the reproduction. But when one gets closer, the differences are obvious. Color, shapes, and even some textures are the same. However, the fact that the original is imbued with the spirit of the painter makes the reproduction a mechanical one: a reproduction devoid of not only human spirit but also all of those characteristics that an artist can relay through the chosen medium.

Music is an even more volatile medium because its creation is almost instantaneous and exists in real time. Music accurately reflects the human ingredients used in its formulation. Conductors who practice inhumanity in various forms end up disguising music to both themselves and their audiences. Just as they are insensitive to others in life, so, too, does their music reflect an artificialness that, unless one is listening closely, is hard to detect. But an audience knows. They know when they have been touched and their lives have been affected. They know the difference between a reproduction and an original creation. They can hear human sincerity in sound. Human

sincerity, love, and caring can be heard in the simplest classroom music to the most complicated symphonic music. They can hear when the composer's intentions are respected and when the ego of the conductor has been substituted for some old-fashioned humility.

Musicians will not be able to allow music to speak in an honest voice if they bring disrespect for the human condition and for people to the podium and, thereby, inflict it upon a composer's handiwork. You can hear this in the music. It is indescribable in a way; the sound is elusive and lacks a depth of texture and color, just like the Giclee prints. Prints are reminders of how great the original work of art was. But a print can never be a substitute for the original.

Musicians must find a way through understanding their relationships with others to discern a "Giclee print" of the music they conduct from an original creation. Great artists have always known the difference in the sounds they make. Depth and interiority that grows out of an unabiding love for all singers, colleagues, friends, and family is the telling ingredient in music making.

"We simply must learn to play together in the same sandbox."

"Pensive Gaze"

Chapter 14

Relationships and the Music Educator

by Kenneth R. Raessler

It is I who must begin....

Once I begin, once I try—here and now, right where I am, not excusing myself by saying that things would be easier elsewhere, without grand speeches and ostentatious gestures, but all the more persistently—to live in harmony with the "voice of Being," as I understand it within myself—as soon as I begin that, I suddenly discover, to my surprise, that I am neither the only one, nor the first, nor the most important one to have set out upon that road....

Whether all is really lost or not depends entirely on whether or not I am lost.... (p. 7)

Václav Havel
Letters to Olga

The topic "relationships" is certainly one of the most important aspects in the private and professional life of music educators. Healthy relationships are essential for success...relationships that nurture energy, create positive environments, and support personal and professional goals. Above all, relationships are the lifeblood of programmatic and professional support. One must be genuine, honest, and candid in relationships, and know when a relationship has changed and for what reason. One learns from relationships.

There are times when music educators are lonely people. While this is sometimes self-inflicted, we do teach a different language. We exist in isolated parts of the building because we "make noise." We may have an itinerant assignment in which we are only in the building for a short period of time. Sometimes we do not want to have relationships with those who are not supportive of us or our programs, but it is essential that we attempt to do so. Music education will never take its place in the school, university, or community if we are not constantly working to develop new personal relationships with our fellow musicians and music teachers, students, peers, administrators, communities, and learners and music consumers of all ages.

knowing thyself

Let us begin by focusing on you in this exercise on building relationships. There are some essentials:

- Be flexible in your teaching, your attitude about teaching, and your attitude about music. Understand that music is just one of many subjects taught. Music is a very important part of learning and the life experience, but not the only part.

- Celebrate the energy inside of you that constitutes who you are, and nurture that energy by connecting it to those who share and appreciate your energy levels.

- Make every effort to function as a pioneer. A pioneer is bold enough to know the difference between complying, growing, and experimenting with change. We frequently experiment with students, but how much do we experiment with ourselves?

- Attempt to define your strengths. Conversely, identify your shortcomings. Knowing who you are and the strengths you have will help you develop relationships that accentuate

148 those strengths and the different personalities with whom you work.

- Understand that there are many things that cannot be changed...history, how people act, the values of others, or the inevitable over which you have no control. It seems worthless to become overly concerned about those things over which you have little or no control, but we do. Rather, it seems more worthwhile to pursue those things we can truly impact.

- Establish your own vision, mission, values, and high-priority goals.

- Think about silence as a worth that brings no risk. It is a marvelous tool! Learn to listen!

- Remember the value of praise—not only to others, but also to yourself. Make sure that relationship with yourself includes an occasional pat on your own back, for the best way to gain the respect of others is to first respect yourself.

We all know it is human nature to favor the underdog, yet human beings love to follow a winner. Relationships must be built to be a winner. When you have given the world the best you have  and still feel unappreciated, then you probably have not helped those with whom you have relationships understand the efforts you have made. When what you have worked so hard to build is destroyed overnight, you must still continue to build and develop relationships. Give the world the best you have anyway, for when positive relationships and skill work together, you can expect a masterpiece. But it is doubtful that a masterpiece in music education, which involves teaching and people and music, can be done without quality relationships.

relationships with students

Relationships with students are built through motivation; inspiration; steady, consistent, and fair discipline; caring; and the ability to laugh and enjoy their unique personalities. Relationships are a powerful part of teaching, one that must be respected and nurtured because it is at the very heart of quality student/teacher relationships. As students experience music at greater levels of depth, sophistication, and understanding, it deepens the relationship the teacher has with them.

J o r d a n   J a m e s [

150

The power you have in your student relationships makes you a considerable force in the school district, the university, or the community. The adults who make the greatest difference in a student's life are not the ones with the most credentials, the most money, or the most awards. Rather, they are the ones who care the most. This requires a level of competence, caring, and honesty that allows you to stand apart from non-music colleagues. When a positive relationship with both students and music is allowed into the arena of learning, we ensure that music will enter the lives of the students and that the music learning will become significant, vital, and exciting.

relationships with peers

Peer relationships are tremendously important. We must work to develop quality relationships with other music colleagues so everyone will willingly work with one another and stand up for advocates of *music*—not just one aspect of the art form. Harmony, blend, and balance are musical goals we all strive for, but are these same qualities not equally as important outside of the classroom or rehearsal hall as you deal with your colleagues? We all know there are individuals who thrive on petty intrigue and vindictive backbiting. We have all likely experienced abuse of student loyalty when students are encouraged to take sides in faculty disputes. This is the antithesis of the quality relationships among peers needed to ensure music program success. Because this is so prevalent, it has as much to do with the fragmentation and fictionalization of our discipline as anything. This simply must not occur...whether in the university or in K–12 music programs.

By training and temperament, music educators are emotional and impassioned about the art they pursue and teach. This often extends into the professional and peer relationships. Could it be that at times we bring the wrong tools to the table to build relationships and solve problems with our colleagues? What stands in good stead in college/university study—the ability to dissect an issue, argue its merits, compete with others, quantify, and criticize—simply does not work in interpersonal situations that require compromise, harmony, and participation in the total process of human interaction.

The emotional and creative passion we bring to music sometimes makes us appear hypersensitive, intellectually arrogant and incredibly selfish. If you do not understand the actions or atti-tudes of another individual, simply ask why rather than speculate behind the person's back. Speculation encourages antagonism that is totally unnecessary and accomplishes nothing. Given the present fragile state of our profession in the educational mainstream, we simply must not foster any sort of curricular fratricide. When these

152

kinds of actions occur, we must remember that our students are put in a no-win situation, and consequently, more losers than winners are created.

If we as musicians and music educators cannot behave with benevolence and civility toward one another, how can we expect our students or anyone else to view us any more kindly? If we cannot reach agreement with one another, how can we expect others to reach agreement with us? To become mature in our relationships is part of being educated rather than merely knowledgeable in a particular area of expertise. Each of us is only as good as all of us, and it is the "all of us" that must come first. We simply must learn to play together in the same sandbox.

relationships with the public

While many of us think we can only communicate with the public, building relationships with the public is also an important element contributing to the success of music education programs. Relationships with the public can take on many delineations; however, these relationships need to be used for more than merely giving out information or manipulating public opinion or reaction. Relationships help establish the values of the program, build an image, bring people together for program

improvement, and communicate success. While relationships with the public are less defined because of the large number of people who must be influenced, there are ways that positive and intimate communications can be used to create positive relationships. The difference between relationships and communication is an interaction between the person and the program...students, directors, faculty, and parents. To be effective in creating support for music education programs, relationships with the public must be rich in human and musical interaction.

153

Finally, the mystique of professional relationships seems complex and complicated in the sheer volume of effort that is demanded. Yet these relationships are a core of music program success and professional recognition, and are an essential component of the activities of leaders who aspire to excel. Done well, the development of these multiple relationships will cause morale to soar, music ensembles and departments to work together more cohesively, and program goals and values to be carefully defined so idealism can flourish. Idealism fosters vision. The philosophy of relationships brought to life by a profession wanting to cultivate these relationships might be just the necessary thrust that will make music programs healthier in schools, districts,

154

universities, and communities. There is really nothing revolutionary presented in this chapter...just plain common sense. But if these relationships were actually employed, the result for music and music education could indeed be revolutionary.

Note: Portions of this chapter are edited from Chapter 5 of *Aspiring to Excel,* also by Kenneth R. Raessler (Chicago: GIA Publications, 2003).

"We've never done it like that before."

"Window to the World"

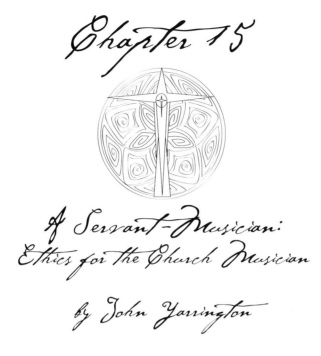

Chapter 15

A Servant-Musician: Ethics for the Church Musician

by John Yarrington

We have come out of the time when obedience, the acceptance of discipline, intelligent courage, and resolution were most important, into that more difficult time when it is a man's duty to understand his world rather than simply fight for it. (p. 74)

Ernest Hemingway

Make Gentle the Life of This World
by Maxwell Taylor Kennedy

Larry Ruddell, who teaches business ethics at Houston Baptist University, suggests identifying potential ethical issues (pitfalls) and that "ethics" is simply the application to a field of what one does and how one does it in a leadership role.

158   We who deal with singers, whether in school or church, have tremendous responsibility because of the nature of our interaction in producing a musical ensemble. "Morality" has to do with right conduct. Singers place their trust in our musical expertise, but more than that, they invest time and energy in a community of music makers, led by someone whose primary concern is not the music making but the music makers. In other words, we should have the highest standards of music making; employ our utmost in study and preparation; have vision for exciting, fulfilling musical experiences. But unless we care about those who *make* the music, we might be described as unethical.

Let me outline three models I have observed. The first model is the *"maestro."* This is the conductor who, with the highest standards described above, operates in an atmosphere of fear. A singer who is thirty seconds late is followed to his/her seat and embarrassed. Others who arrive sans pencil or score are also singled out for public humiliation.

This type of individual almost always needs a scapegoat on which to vent personal frustration or anxiety. I have often seen this during the dress rehearsal before a concert. Someone who came in late, cut off early, didn't look up, or processed into the wrong spot was singled out for abuse during the entire rehearsal. Everyone knew that someone was going to be "it," but exactly who was always left to chance. In the context of this chapter, is this "ethical behavior"? Resoundingly, it is not! Is it accepted? Often, it is. Those who want to sing in the "top" group or play on the "varsity" often submit to this behavior that amounts, in my judgment, to abuse.

The second model is the *"nice" approach.* Afraid to ask for any standards of musical correctness or rehearsal faithfulness, this conductor settles for less in a rather humiliating environment. Once chorus members realize they can be late or absent and still be allowed to sing, whether in concert or in church, they will take full advantage. Often, this manifests itself in church. The problem is that the musical offering suffers, the conductor suffers, and the members of the choir who are regular and want more also suffer. The fear is that if the conductor asks for attendance responsibility or growth in singing beautiful vowels and articulating consonants, people will be "run off." Worse is the notion that working on the principles of good choral ensemble is somehow "un-Christian." Is this ethical behavior? Does it represent respect for the time and talents of those who volunteer to come and to sing? Resoundingly, it does not!

The third model is a *hybrid of the first two models:* seeking the highest standards of choral performance while caring about and nurturing the performers. For me, this means creating a climate in which everyone is encouraged to do his/her best in the service of the music. Attendance is enforced, marking is encouraged, sectional rehearsals are expected, good singing habits are taught, and understanding is fostered so the culminating product represents an amalgam of all the best talent and interest in the room.

As Robert Shaw once said, "When I conduct, I attempt to contact all of the intelligence in the room." I believe that, ethically, this third model is the most effective over time. We can love the people while working on the product. But how does one value each individual person as the demands of ensemble are being made? Can one achieve an outstanding product while nurturing, loving, caring for the individuals making up that product? I believe both the individual value and the demands of the musical product can be satisfied. So the answer is, resoundingly, yes.

Harold Best, in *Music Through the Eyes of Faith,* puts it this way: "What does it mean to be creative in our music making? Above all, it means that we should not make music to prove that we are or to authenticate ourselves. God created in us the capability for understanding that we are authenticated in him, not in what we do. In the final analysis, music making is neither a means nor an end, but an offering, therefore an act of worship."[1] All music makers everywhere must understand this and proceed accordingly. Nothing but harm lies ahead if we try to authenticate ourselves with our musical works or become so attached to them—*addicted* might be a better word—that we have no sense of worth or being without this

"proof" of our existence.

Each musician must come to experience the dignity, rightness, and eventual joy of putting things aside, of emptying oneself and taking the form of a servant. Such musicians must be able to move back and forth gracefully, servingly, willingly, from the symphony to the folk tune, back and forth without complaint, compromise, or snobbery, without the conceit that doing an oratorio is somehow more worthy or more deserving than doing a hymn tune. All servant musicians must be able to be in creative transit, serving this community and challenging that one, all the while showing grace, power, elegance, and imagination. (p. 33)

1. See yourself as the church's "song" leader.

2. Find opportunity to lead singing at:

    a. Board meetings

    b. Committee meetings

    c. Sunday school

    d. Vacation Bible school

    e. Summer "Gospel Series"

    f. Hymn sings

3. Strive for flexibility, but don't be a doormat.

4. Be a friend to your youth director, Christian education director, organist, and minister.

5. Make friends with your custodians; know their names.

6. Calendar conflicts are a major source of irritation. Be on the solution side. Look ahead, anticipate problems, and be the problem-solver.

7. If you can answer the question, "Who are the hymns for?" then you are on the road to success. Find creative ways to involve the congregation:

    a. Calls to worship, prayer, benediction responses

    b. Different doxological responses

    c. Hymn anthems

    d. Do not tell them anything about Ralph Vaughan-Williams; they don't care. Sing to them—they sing back to you.

    e. Do approach them with love, expectation, and good humor.

    f. Know your denominational hymnal and supplements, as well as others.

    g. Use "appropriate" ("suitable") rather than "good" or "bad."

    h. Allow your people to sing songs they know and like. They don't all have to be the best musically or the most outstanding theologically.

8. Be smart in dealing with music committees: Don't get "artsy" with them. Deal in facts: "We would be better served to purchase a pipe organ than an electronic one because, once purchased, maintenance costs are reduced and life expectancy is greater."

9. You don't have to sacrifice the demands of music on the altar of ministry; the tension, however, is great.

10. You are not superhuman. Sit lightly with yourself. Laugh often—fifteen belly laughs a day is minimum; otherwise, you are "under-laughed."

11. The strangest folk make their way to your choir. Be ready for them, love them, nurture them. Expect the best of them and be patient. Choir is the place where the weird, the malcontent, the troubled, the strange find a home along with the rest of your more or less normal singers. Make a place for everyone, but remember that you may have to step in for the good of the whole at some point.

12. Don't be afraid to hug someone, but do be sensitive to body language that says "No hug"! Do send personal notes. Even on mimeographed letters, add a personal sentence at the bottom. Do go to the hospital, the funeral home, etc.

If you are a young person going into church work, you are embarking on a wonderful journey, but one that is fraught with challenge. Remember:

- Take your time.

- Get to know your people personally.

- Don't be afraid to ask for the highest standards from everyone.

- Know that some won't and some can't do what you wish.

164

- Be positive.

- Be a teacher who studies and then finds many ways to involve choir members and congregation alike in the community of singing.

Your relationships with staff, especially the ministerial staff, are crucial. Again, if you see yourself as the congregational song leader, not the director of artistic standards, you will be better served. Most of the ministers with whom you work have had very little coursework in liturgy or hymnology. Because you have had this training, you can guide, encourage, educate (carefully), and be a resource person for your clergy. Here is what I say: "The hymns are not mine." Your flexibility when the pastor wants a hymn below the "artistic standards" set in your music school or seminary will pay big dividends. When you know your own hymnal, you can suggest alternatives in a positive, helpful, nonjudgmental approach. You don't have to "slum." You just have to be willing to take the long view and constantly interject alternative choices.

Provide opportunities for those who wish to make tangible contributions to your program. Handbells, hymnals, robes, music stands, stand lights, etc., make wonderful memorials. Encourage purchase of an anthem in honor or memory of someone, and personalize the box or the individual copies. Always have a list of anthems you wish to add to the library, and attempt to suit the needs of the "donee" to the wants of the "director-ee."

Here are some pitfalls:

- Don't take someone's piano unseen. Have a tuner check it first.

- "Susie plays the flute." Yes, she plays. No, she doesn't play well.

- Don't get caught in the wedding music triangle. If you and the pastoral staff are not clear about what is "appropriate," you will have endless trouble. This is always a pastoral, not a musical, decision.

- "If I know the anthem for Sunday, I think I should be allowed to sing even if I miss the rehearsal."

  Response you should give: "We need you at the rehearsal because you can lead the others."

  Response you'd like to give: "I hope you find a choir that operates that way."

- "Why don't we sing the hymns we know"?

  Response you should give: "I keep a list from Sunday to Sunday. Let's sit down and look over that."

  Response you'd like to give: "I sweat blood over hymn choice. How dare you question it."

- "Can the organist play softer"?

  Response: "Yes."

- "Do you know you have a child singing low."

  Response you should give: "I didn't hear that, but thanks for pointing it out."

  Response you'd like to give: "If you knew how hard I have worked with Johnnie to get him on pitch...."

Take time for you. Start your day with Scripture and prayer. Pray by name for people, especially the troublesome ones. Find a colleague (in another church or in another city) with whom you can communicate. You will find that many problems are the same and not unique to your situation. Read and study. Start with *The Musicians Soul* (1999) by James Jordan and any other publications by him.

Study your music, and as Helen Kemp said, "Play your work/work your plan." Be smart in scheduling. Variety of style and difficulty makes your job easier. Time your rehearsals, especially the ones with children or youth. Make rehearsals fun; make them challenging. Remember the three "Rs" of teaching: repeat—repeat—repeat. The better your study, the more creative your teaching. Always approach what you do in expectation of the best.

In church, you will find some of the worst attitudes and the most uncaring, un-Christian behavior. It will seem to you, at times, that the best folks are outside the environs of church. Give up the notion that you can "fix" every situation or that everyone will both like you and respond to what you are doing. (I give much better advice than I take).

Remember: There is no such thing as "constructive criticism." Also   **167**
remember: Everyone is a "music critic." "I know what I like" usually
means "I *like* what I *know*."

The seven last words of the church—"We've never done it like
that before"—will always be present, but for the most part, you will
rise above this. Sometimes, however, you will be tempted to jump out
of your office window. Remember that you are only on the second
floor—hardly worth it!

note

1. Harold Best, *Music through the Eyes of Faith* (New York: HarperCollins
   Publishers, Inc., 1993), 14–5.

"It is a daily yearning to work with his hands that gives insight."

"Totem 11"

Chapter 16

The Role of Humility on the Journey

"I guess this has always been part of my nature," says Noble, who admits that only lately did he realize there was a janitor inside him just dying to get out. "This is my form of jogging and there is such a wonderful sense of accomplishment. The time goes so fast. One would wonder what would occupy the mind at this time, but you are totally absorbed in it. I guess it's just that you're always looking for something."

In a way, that's comforting to Noble. He does not deny that, maybe someday, this could lead to a whole new career. "I know I could be happy as a custodian," he says. "It's that element of service, making people happy. Ever since the seventh grade one of my life's desires has been to be a waiter." (pp. 134–135)

Wilfred F. Bunge

Warmly, Weston: A Luther College Life

170

This is why, in an act of imitation, every afternoon that I am at home finds me in my backyard for fifteen minutes tending to what has become the fourth component of my daily spiritual practice. For as long as I can remember that practice begins, on arising, with hatha-yoga for the body, a reading from a religious classic for my mind, and a blend of prayer and meditation for my spirit. Those three practices remain in place, but it helps to have them grounded, and that is what the addition of composting accomplishes. Being physically anchored to the earth helps us to keep my ego from bobbing along mindlessly on the sea of life. (p. 210)

Huston Smith

The Way Things Are

It came to me that the soul is like a castle made exclusively of diamond or some other very clear crystal. In this castle are a multitude of dwellings, just as in heavens there are many mansions. (p. 35)

St. Teresa of Avila

The Interior Castle

Art is not a pastime but a priesthood. (p. 119)

Jean Cocteau

Walking in This World by Julia Cameron

Always the wish that you may find patience enough in yourself to endure, and simplicity enough to believe; that you may acquire more and more confidence in that which is difficult, and in your solitude among others. (p. 120)

Rainer Maria Rilke

Walking in This World by Julia Cameron

Humility can be both a curse and a blessing, and the same can be said for ego, too. Flexibility or firmness, gentle concern or ruthless determination, collaboration or competition: which is more important, which will contribute most to our music making? Do we even have a choice?

Egotistical behavior can alienate, antagonize, and polarize those around you, isolate you, and even help you to lose your job; and yet every artist I have interviewed feels that a healthy ego is essential to artistry. The question remains: how do we strike a healthy balance between humility and ego? (p. 225)

When you use ego to compete against another person rather than striving within yourself, the game changes from an Inner Game of artistry to an Outer Game of "beat the competition"—and that's not a game you can ever really win, because it zaps your energy, it takes your attention away from the music. (p. 234)

Barry Green

The Mastery of Music

I am not sure I have explained this well. Self-knowledge is so important that I do not care how high you are raised up to the heavens. I never want you to cease cultivating it. As long as we are on this earth, there is nothing more essential than humility. Enter the room of self-knowledge first, instead of floating to other places. This is the path. Traveling along a safe and level road, who needs wings to fly? Let's make the best possible use of our feet first and learn to know ourselves. (p. 46)

Do you think that your deep humility, your self-sacrifice, your bountiful charity and commitment to being of service to all beings meaningless? (p. 294)

St. Teresa of Avila

The Interior Castle

As I recently meditated on the term *mudra,* I became particularly aware of the symbol of a lock. A lock always conceals a secret. We frequently use gestures in an unconscious way to seal something, for example, when giving special weight to a decision, or reaching an agreement with another person, or even with cosmic consciousness. In precisely the same way, we may also seal something with our inner forces—we reach an understanding with ourselves. (p. 3)

The outer circumstances of our lives usually shape themselves according to our imagination and the contents of our minds. So we have the possibility of shaping our inner images in such a way that we enjoy life, experience success in our work, and have relationships on a loving and understanding basis. It is very important to create an unshakable faith and be filled with both fervor and serenity to accompany our self-made images. We need to create little experiences

Walk s'naicisuM ehT

of success for ourselves, since what functions in a small way will also succeed on a larger scale. (p. 15)

Gertrud Hirschi

Mudras: Yoga in Your Hands

*I*f one ponders what feelings are operating when bad or insensitive things happen in artists' lives, one can certainly attest that at those moments, there is a total absence of humility: humility concerning one's own importance to both the world and music; humility concerning the respect and admiration for the gifts and opinions of others; humility concerning the value of every human being.

It has been my experience that artists who assert their ego upon others and the ensemble are, at that moment, in a state of unawareness about their simple little place in the world. The only music that matters is the music "they" make. Many times such artists are so self-absorbed that they never hear the music that is a product of their somewhat distorted and portrayed self. Many great artists that I know and have known always have humility intact and operating. No matter what the circumstance, no matter what the quality of the music they are either rehearsing or performing, they are at all times humble. Their humbleness seems to magnify the good people and the good sounds around them.

It strikes me that if one does not come with humility naturally, then it can be both learned and practiced. The following story touched me deeply and further convinced me that the daily practice of humility should be part of the musician's walk.

Trash Is "Refreshing"

"I have a need to replenish myself, especially emotionally," says Noble, who claims that gathering debris is his R and R. "I do a lot of traveling and teaching and rehearsing and expend a lot of emotional energy. Picking up trash is totally physical so it is bound to be refreshing."

And educational, too, he's quick to add. Noble's garbage expeditions on one college site where fires had destroyed buildings in 1889 and 1942 led him to some stunning speculations on man's relationship with trash, from past to present.

"I was amazed by the amount of Noxzema used and you must remember this was a men's dorm," he says, shaking his head in bewilderment. " I don't really know what that means."

He says today, plastic is the most prevalent form of refuse, that fewer and fewer cigarette packages are found and that he can tell when students are approaching mid-terms or finals from all the broken glass around.

"I haven't made a scientific study, but during the pressure points of the college year you are more apt to find broken glass," he explains, "I think you can see how that is a result of student frustration."

No theories are available on why the false teeth wound up under some trees. Or how the stop sign made its way to the bottom of a ravine. Or the reasons behind all those watches, keys, hunting boots, shoes and socks, letters (he never reads them) and money that Noble has hauled off in his rounds which often begin at dawn.

"I sometimes wonder what the campus janitors think when they see these trash cans just full of all this unusual stuff," says Noble.

It was estimated that he has put in 210 hours in his clean-up campaign that has covered half of the hills surrounding the campus, the football stadium, a city park and sidewalks to and from his home. After beginning his treks with only a small shopping bag, he now has graduated to carrying large cans he gets from the school cafeteria.

"I guess this has always been part of my nature," says Noble, who admits that only lately did he realize there was a janitor inside him just dying to get out." This is my form of jogging and there is such a wonderful sense of accomplishment. The time goes so fast. One would wonder what would occupy the mind at this time, but you are totally absorbed in it. I guess it's just that you're always looking for something."

In a way, that's comforting to Noble. He does not deny that, maybe someday, this could lead to a whole new career.

"I know that I could be happy as a custodian," he says. "It's that element of service, making people happy. Ever since the seventh grade one of my life's desires has been to be a waiter."

Noble's family might not be nearly so surprised to learn of his janitorial ambitions. After all, he was the only one who never had to be told to clean up his room.

Wilfred F. Bunge

Warmly, Weston: A Luther College Life

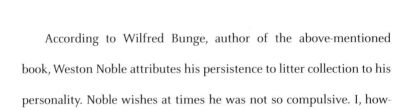

According to Wilfred Bunge, author of the above-mentioned book, Weston Noble attributes his persistence to litter collection to his personality. Noble wishes at times he was not so compulsive. I, however, have another theory, perhaps a theory that resonates in the souls of all great artists.

At first when I heard this story, I was a bit shocked and was very taken aback. Here was a conductor who I hold in the highest regard whose major pastime is picking up trash! I couldn't believe it. This quiet, gentle soul who makes such beautiful and honest music spends the beginning of his days gathering campus debris.

My first thought was, "This is a bit abnormal." But then I read the story again and began to understand why we might all consider engaging in such an activity. Musicians as a group have an almost inherited tendency to elevate themselves in their own minds as "being better" than others, and when it is necessary, they forcefully inflict themselves upon others. The justifications are almost always "for the music." Humility and humbleness are nowhere to be found—just omnipresent ego and oppressive energies with the role of stifling the spirits of all those around. Such persons at no time in their lives practice some form of personal humility.

Imagine...Weston Noble, one of this century's greatest choral conductors and spirits, does not think so highly of himself that he would not pick up trash. How many "great artists" do you know who would do this, or anything that even resembles this? I believe one of the reasons Weston has done this for years is that, for some reason, the feeling of service that is coupled with a certain kind of humbleness brings incredible peace and calm to his soul and his daily routine. He practices a form of humility every day.

I recently saw a beautiful photographic essay of the Trappist Monks in Spencer, Massachusetts, which showed the cloakroom for their work clothes. Their garb for their work day, working in the fields at these seemingly "mundane" tasks, serves to both ground them and invest them in a type of humbleness that

Photo by Br. Emmanuel Morinelli, O.C.S.O.

only working with one's hands can impart. Perhaps one reason why artists lack human skills of humility, compassion, and love as they make music is because they do not engage in any activity that places them in a true service and serving capacity. To garden, plant, clean streets, pick up trash, or volunteer to work in a food kitchen might all serve to keep one in touch with one's innate and humble "core."

The great artists I have known have a remarkable humility about what they do. They believe that they possess no unique gifts other than a love and passion for making music. Humbleness is a daily part of their lives in some way, and that presence of humbleness carries over into their music and their way of relating to others.

I was thinking about great teachers of mine who used humbleness as the medium of instruction. I could think of many, but one stood out. Sarah Farley was my third grade teacher. A stocky and gruff woman, she was one of my favorite teachers. She was very good at teaching the things of third grade. But every day in that class, she talked to us tiny third graders about sharing—sharing ourselves and what we had with others. Sharing of all types received lavish praise in her classroom. In fact, the entire school year was a study in sharing with others. Imagine, a third grade course in humility through sharing at that very impressionable age. I remember to this day how good it felt to give something you made to others, or how it was good to share your lunch with someone in the class who had less than you, or how it was good to do without so others could have. We cleaned every day! The teacher told us how it was noble to be in service of others. I vividly recall how beautiful I felt every day of that school year. I also recall how none of us in the class fought with each other and how we all perceived each other as equals. In that class, we never had individual projects. They were always group projects, and we were taught that we were all equal. That year was an incredible experience in humility in service to others—not yourself.

Some of the greatest artists have existed at the poverty level while they made great art. For example, the stories of the destitute and humble existence of Béla Bartók are legendary. Mother Teresa lived a bare life in service of a higher good. Many great musicians grew up in humble beginnings early in their lives. My father was a self-employed auto mechanic. I watched him every day labor in dirt and grease to repair cars and make a living. I never heard him complain or want for something better in his life. An orphan, I am certain my father knew humility. Manual labor was a noble task; it was his way of serving. He was always thankful to be able to make a living that way. And through his garage, he not only repaired cars, but I was witness to countless acts of kindness.

The story about Weston Noble also made me ponder the relationship of the work of one's hands and its intimate connection with humility and humbleness. Hands have a unique way of connecting one to their humble core. In fact, many believe it is through the hands that one maintains contact with the elemental world. In hatha-yoga, there are twenty-five mudras—that is, hand, body, and eye positions. In a book entitled *Mudras: Yoga in Your Hands,* Gertrud Hirschi writes that through a practice of "hand yoga," one can gain understanding of one's oneness and humanity within a larger world—a type of humility? When we gain an understanding of our inner forces, we gain an understanding of both ourselves and others.

So at the core of Weston's trash gathering is much more than an eccentric habit. It is his own type of Yoga mudra. It is work with his hands. It is a daily yearning to work with his hands that gives him insight into himself. Picking up trash calms him and gives him solace. Through that act, his soul refreshes its humility daily. That humility then plays a pivotal role in his teaching and music making each day.

Part of the musician's walk should perhaps be a daily and planned task that keeps one grounded and humble. Such well-spent time will, no doubt, yield great music and great art for each of us.

"Acknowledging our self-worth is an important step toward connection."

"Reverence"

Chapter 17

Women: Mimetics and Self-Perception

by Allegra Martin

*D*r. Jordan asked me to choose an idea from his previous books and use that as a starting point for reflection on challenges I have faced as a conducting student. When I read about mimetics, I was reminded of my favorite tae kwon do parable, which I read several years ago while studying for my black belt exam and have paraphrased here:

Once upon a time, there was a meeting of several renowned martial arts teachers. They all studied different styles and rarely interacted with each other. Some of them had never even met. But on this particular occasion, they decided to travel to meet with each other on top of a mountain. They each brought along several of their top students so the students could see something of the world—and hopefully learn from the experience.

When they arrived, the students were told to wait at the bottom of the mountain until the conference was over. Since all of the students were waiting in the same place, they naturally began discussing their different styles. One student would demonstrate a technique and boast about its effectiveness. Then several others would say, "No, no! We have something completely different, and much better!" All the students ended up arguing, each trying to impress the others with the superiority of their own style.

Meanwhile on top of the mountain, the old masters were having a delightful time. "We have a technique that goes like this," one would say. Then the others would all nod and say, "Yes, yes, we have something very similar to that! It looks a little different, but the purpose is exactly the same!" Then they all beamed at each other, fascinated that their disparate arts were, at their cores, so similar.

I have always loved this parable, and the metaphor can be applied even more broadly. Not only do different martial arts (such as tae kwon do and karate) have deeply rooted similarities, but also completely different fields of study (such as martial arts and conducting) have many *philosophical* similarities. In my study of conducting, as in my study of tae kwon do, the deeper I go the more familiar the territory becomes and the more often I run into the same problems. Over the past year, the primary problem I have had with

klaW s'naisiuM ehT

my conducting is the same problem I have had for years when sparring: I have a deep fear of causing offense. In both conducting and tae kwon do, fear of "ruffling feathers" can be crippling. I believe I am not alone in this fear, and as a woman, the culture I am part of reinforces my instinct to avoid causing discomfort.

It is a curious fact that when learning to spar in tae kwon do, women tend to apologize every time a punch or kick makes contact, even though making contact is the goal in a sparring match. We apologize even when we miss. "I'm sorry, I'm sorry," is a constant refrain. Apparently, women are far more terrified of causing damage than men, who only apologize profusely when sparring women. Women apologize to everyone. Locker room interactions follow a similar self-denigrating pattern. "You sparred so well today!" "Oh, no, I'm really terrible. Did you see that roundhouse kick? It was awful. And I couldn't move at all!" "Oh, no, you were really good. I'm so much slower than you are!" Even when compliments are given in an honest, supportive spirit, they tend to be phrased at the giver's expense.

I know because I do this myself, all the time. By now, I am extremely sensitive to it, and yet the apology slips out whenever I think I might have kicked someone a little too hard. No matter how I resolve before a match that I will *not* apologize for anything until the match is over, I never succeed. Likewise, it is surprisingly difficult to

186 give myself the respect I deserve in conversations off the mat. When I compliment others, I am sometimes hurt if they contradict me because I was honestly trying to tell them they had done well. Therefore, I try to accept compliments graciously when someone tells me I fought well, but the effort of not saying, "Oh, no, I was terrible," is sometimes almost painfully uncomfortable. Simply saying, "Thank you!" and smiling can be harder than fighting the match.

I was never aware of this tendency towards apology until I began tae kwon do, but then I started to notice myself apologizing frequently. If someone bumps into me on the street, I automatically apologize. And I am not the only one. I notice many women of my acquaintance automatically apologizing for things or downplaying their accomplishments so as not to make other people uncomfortable by their skill or intelligence.

I was talking to a friend of mine about this tendency towards apology, and she told me the following remarkable story.

After college, I started taking public transit daily. I noticed that men in the subway seemed to walk right into me quite often and got the impression I was missing some sort of signal. They almost always seemed surprised and apologized. Then I realized they were shouldering me or hitting me with bags because they had full faith I would step out of the way. I thought this was a personal blind spot on my part, a bit of social ineptness. It is, in some ways, but not like I thought.

About two years ago, I was reading a book about transgender issues, especially transsexuals and issues about permanent transitioning from one sex to another. I remember clearly some first-person accounts of folks who help male-to-female transsexuals transition. Apparently, one of the hardest things for someone who was raised a boy to learn about public comportment for women is stepping out of the way of men who are walking directly towards you. Men, in general, pick a direction and walk it, and if another man is in the way, they do the same little negotiation dance two women will do. If a woman is walking in a path that crosses a man's, she tends to step aside and he tends to act like he expects her to.

The reasons for this difference between the sexes could be argued into infinity. Some would argue that nature is responsible—that women, being more skilled at communication, are more sensitive to the ways in which they might cause offense. Others, myself included, would argue that it is because of nurturing—that our culture teaches women not to make other people uncomfortable, to consider the feelings of others before themselves, and not to make themselves targets by being too impressive or admirable. But why do so many people choose to act this way in the first place? Why is it that I instinctively believe that downplaying my skills will endear me to others? The answer lies in mimetic theory.

188   Readers of James Jordan's previous books will already be familiar with mimetics. Briefly, mimetics is the theory of envy, as developed by Réné Girard. Mimetics postulates that we must constantly, consciously fight our instinctive envious responses towards others to ensure healthy relationships. In the world of music—where what you do and how you sound is so hard to separate from who you are—mimetics is a powerful determinant of people's interactions. But while most of mimetic theory addresses eliminating envy in ourselves, there is also the powerful question of how we respond to envy, real or perceived, in others.

I believe that humans intuit, subconsciously, the entire mimetic theory. We know that people may get envious of us if we are obviously skilled at something, or talented, or powerful, or beautiful. Therefore, we downplay and undercut our skills and gifts to prevent a negative mimetic response directed towards us. It is not done out of subconscious concern for the other person. It is done for our own benefit, to prevent negative emotions being directed our way. Why else do we (especially, as I have described, women) so instinctively not stand up and take joy in our accomplishments? We are scared that others will not love us if we shine too bright; we are afraid that if they think we are "better" than they are, they will not like us, they will be angry...because they are envious.

In some small way, our instincts are correct. If I am hired for a great conducting position that a friend of mine wanted, my friend will envy me, which might negatively impact our interactions temporarily. The reverse is also true: Just as we feel cool towards those in positions of power who we envy, we unconsciously warm towards those at a disadvantage. If a Little League team of eight-year-olds goes up against a team of twelve-year-olds, everyone will root for the eight-year-olds because everyone likes an underdog. But because our attitudes have a concrete impact on what we are able to achieve, going into a tae kwon do match with an apologetic manner and a desire to not make the other person feel bad so he/she will still like us is pretty much a recipe for crushing defeat. Likewise, standing on the conductor's podium and hoping to avoid causing offense is equally self-defeating.

It took me a year of conducting study to realize that the problem that had so dogged me in tae kwon do was equally crippling in music. I would receive criticism on my poor posture and my inability to communicate clearly, but it took a while to realize the root of the problem. My back was rounded and my shoulders hunched slightly forward because I was unconsciously try-ing to adapt an ingratiating posture. I was afraid to stand up straight because I felt it created a cold distance between me and the singers. I was afraid to communicate because I didn't want to step on anyone's toes—if their interpretation was different than mine, I didn't want to

190

impose my will on them and insult their musicality. I didn't want the singers to think I was proud, or snobby, or disinterested in them as people with individual opinions.

Of course, I was also failing to do my job. Who will have an opinion if I don't? My attitude is mirrored in the attitude of the chorus. If I am confident in my performance, then I am giving permission for the musicians to be confident as well. I do not have to be everyone's friend, and probably not everyone will like me, but the chorus wants and expects me to lead them. By trying not to offend the singers, I was sabotaging myself before I stepped onto the podium, and more importantly, I was sabotaging the chorus. My insecurity was transferred to them, and they were denied the chance to sing as boldly and musically as possible.

Realizing there is a problem, of course, is not the same as fixing the problem. I still have a lot of work to do, both on the mat and on the podium. But the first step is realizing and admitting that I am afraid of success because I am afraid others will dislike me for it. Only when I face this fact can I begin to succeed. By understanding the reasons behind my fears, I can begin to address them. As Marianne Williamson, co-leader of the United States Department of Peace movement, said:

Our deepest fear is not that we are inadequate. Our deepest
fear is that we are powerful beyond measure. It is our light,
not our darkness that most frightens us...And as we let our
own light shine, we unconsciously give other people permission to do the same.

My journey over the past year has led me to become more
comfortable with my own power. I hope that my increasing
confidence will enable my singers to embrace their power as well.
While we may fear that power will distance us from each other,
acknowledging our self-worth is an important step toward connection
and, ultimately, honest music making.

"There is something about putting pen to paper that compels honest reflection.

"Bell Rock

Chapter 18

The Musician's Need to Journal Daily: Being Aware of the Herd

"Absence, absence": a poet hears the cry. Winterly frost comes in the void left when love dies or a lover grows distant. Let a new love come into life or let the enduring one come close again and summer can return to the heart. So it is with human affairs. The absence can also come, however, to a waste space left when the divine is distant, the sacred is remote, when God is silent. The wind of furious winter for a while blows without and then grows silent as spring comes. The fury and the bleakness within the soul can remain, no matter what the season or the weather. (p. 2)

My address, then, to the wintry sort of spiritual hearts is based, at rock bottom and boldly, on texts. Italicize the word *texts* and use it again, my notes say, to be sure that no one mistakes the character of this caring. Risk losing attention over something so seemingly banal as a word about texts. Yet the risk can have rewards. Winston Churchill once said that a person can confront a truth a thousand times and not notice it, and on the one thousand and first occasion can stumble over it. The reality becomes alive; it reinforces itself. Whether we are here talking about truth is secondary to the fact that we are locating a reality. Wintry sorts of spirituality can find nurture through texts. (p. 28)

Martin E. Marty

A   C r y   o f   A b s e n c e

Ethos, from which we get the word *ethics,* originally meant a place where animals frequent. When we herd together, how do we behave? Do we look after one another? Do we take care of the place where we gather—the land, the city, the drinking water? Are we welcome here? Can we be ourselves? These are basic questions of human existence, and how we answer them and live them has everything to do with our ethics. (p. 214)

Ethics is a way of recognizing that although we are each alone in this universe, we are all alone together. We can make a good life not only by protecting each other but by being creative together and taking our pleasures from one another. (pp. 215–216)

Thomas Moore

T h e   S o u l ' s   R e l i g i o n

Life is incredibly important, and one must try to cherish every minute. Since I changed my religion, I don't think I've made any leaps in character. When asked if my Jewish faith helped me cope with my MS I always reply, to be quite honest, not as much as music, because for me the Judaism is almost bound up in the music. I just cannot separate them or indicate their boundaries. I know through all my troubles, I could never say that I am not a lucky person, because I am blessed. (pp. 130–131)

195

Jacqueline du Pré
The Mastery of Music by Barry Green

For many of us, it is hard to be both large enough and small enough to hold the range of life. Without a spiritual connection to something larger than ourselves, we lose our bearings, our beings, our sense of scale. Of course we do. The human experience is intricate, painful, and very beautiful. We lead lives filled with loss and filled with gain. Without a tool to metabolize what we live through—and for me that tool is Morning Pages—and even with it, it is hard to process who we have been and who we have become. So much happens to each of us. It is hard to make peace. Life is like the sea. A wave of memory sweeps in that threatens to overwhelm us and then the wave retreats, leaving us to wonder what has been washed ashore. (p. 34)

In the midst of personal drama, it can be harder to hold our creative grid. We may be tempted to binge on phone time or lengthy heartfelt conversations across the kitchen table over cups of tea. Drama is seductive, and artists must learn to not be readily seduced. Our work must be sacrosanct, and if it isn't, drama soon seeps into our  personalities. We feel ill tempered and out of sorts. The world goes off-kilter and it tends to stay there until we get back to working. (p. 102)

Julia Cameron
The Sound of Paper

196 Today many people live the external life exclusively, and when the inner world erupts or stirs, they rush to a therapist or druggist for help. They try to explain the profound mythic developments in the language of behavior and experience. Often, they have no idea what is happening to them, because they have been so cut off from the deep self. Their own soul is so alien to them that they are unaware of what is going on outside the known realm of fact.

Former methods of keeping in touch with the inner life have gone out of mode. Diaries, letters and deep conversations help focus attention on developments and materials that lie beneath the surface. Only one hundred years ago, without benefit of typewriters and processors, people kept elaborate, long and detailed diaries and notebooks. We seem to have left behind these methods of reflection in favor of technologies for action. (pp. 4–5)

Thomas Moore

The Original Self

Modern thinking has often lost its way by separating the problem of truth from the problem of living, cognition from man's total situation. Such separation has resulted in reason's isolationism, in utopian and irrelevant conceptions of man. Reflection alone will not procure self-understanding. The human situation is disclosed in the thick of living. The deed is the distillation of the self. We can display no initiative, no freedom in sheer being; our responsibility is in living. (p. 94)

Abraham Joshua Heschel

W h o   I s   M a n ?

*A*t a recent dinner with Weston Noble, he relayed to me his daily practice of journaling. Each day, he reflects on what has transpired and records the events of the day in his journal. Those events that he feels he could have approached or handled better he writes in red. The rest of the day's events are written in blue. The red entries he then tries to correct the next day. What is more important is that he does not miss a single day. His journal is an ongoing record of his daily awarenesses and unawarenesses—an objective recording of each day's major events that provides material for thought and reflection.

What strikes me as particularly unique about this practice is that many musicians and teachers likely do not objectively analyze both the great occurrences and the not-so-great stumbles throughout each day. I have noticed that, left unattended, the great occurrences become fewer and fewer as time goes on, and the "stumbles" tend to repeat themselves and almost multiply in an exponential fashion. I suppose this all has to do with a certain lack of accountability in what we do on a daily basis. Because of the impact musicians play in the lives of others, I believe we have a moral responsibility to journal. While recognition of problems is relatively easy, the correcting of those problems requires more commitment.

Later in this book, I talk about ethics and ethical codes. The word "ethics" comes from the root word "ethos," which means *herd* or

Photo by Br. Emmanuel Morinelli, O.C.S.O.

group. Ethical codes are "rules" or corrections in course that improve our lot with all those with whom we deal and experience life and music on a daily basis. It seems that it would be difficult to arrive at an ethical code without having the ability to step back from one's life and profession to objectively analyze how one has interacted with the "herd."

Codes of ethics can be rigid, or they can be vibrantly alive because they constantly change to improve the experience of the "herd." In thinking about Weston Noble's daily ritual, we must step back and admire his commitment not only to himself, but to his herd.

He holds himself accountable on a daily basis for his treatment of others, both within musical situations and outside of his ensemble experiences. This is not only admirable, but remarkable. What is even more remarkable is that someone who is in the eighth decade of his life cares deeply enough about others to constantly re-evaluate his human interactions. I have experienced persons firsthand who I am confident have never reflected upon what they have done to others and have no sense of responsibility to the "herd." And if I had journaled in this manner in the early part of my career, there would have been many days when most of my writing would have been in red.

Musicians, especially conductors and teachers, should journal daily and perhaps devote a few minutes to reflective note taking after a rehearsal. Journaling is not a new concept. Julia Cameron in her books on creativity has moved artists to consider their "daily pages." Saint Augustine recorded his daily reflections in journals. Martin Luther kept what amounted to logs of his daily thoughts, as did Abraham Lincoln. In fact, many of the great persons of the human race journaled. The Da Vinci journals record not only his creative ideas but also the mental struggles he endured as he wrestled with solving scientific issues.

Others have felt more comfortable writing their "journals" in the form of a letter. The letters of Robert Shaw to his choruses are legend, as are the letters Leonard Bernstein lovingly wrote to The New York

200

Philharmonic. Winston Churchill used a diary to help him reflect and ponder the results of his actions.

There is something about putting pen to paper that compels honest reflection—not computer-generated, word processed diaries. Direct connection of pen to paper creates a different reality—a very personal time when no machine intercedes. Writing also, by its very nature, takes longer. Many of us now type almost faster than we think. Writing a journal allows our mind to operate at a reflective speed, a certain kind of honest not possible with a computer.

So begin to journal daily. Perhaps start by just journaling only about your rehearsals and then, if time permits, about the day. In addition to journaling, you might also write a short story about an event each day. Martin Marty, in his book on psalms, remarks that the psalms are reflective texts (or journals, if you may) based upon the psalmists' struggles as human experiences.

Journaling can provide for a continual refining of our life with the "herd." There can be no more important task in life than continuing to improve on our ability to love and care for others, especially within the world of a musical ensemble.

"Ethical character is built one behavior at a time."

"Placed Sphere"

Chapter 19

Ethics and the Music Educator

by Kenneth R. Raessler

"The pursuit of truth" rightly implies that a gap exists between our-selves and truth. But what's hidden and evasive? Is it we or truth? Maybe it is we who evade truth's quest for us. (p. 119)

William Sloane Coffin
Credo

In the final analysis, we count for something only because of the essential we embody, and if we do not embody that, life is wasted. (p. x)

C. G. Jung

The Soul's Code by James Hillman

*Y*ogi Berra was once asked what he would do if he found $1,000,000 that someone had lost. He replied, "If the guy was real poor, I'd give it back to him." I know, the ethics of a music educator has nothing to do with sports or a sports figure. Or does it? Based on my observations, the topic of ethics with regard to the music profession is not a very popular one. As I began writing this chapter, I found virtually no material to work with. It just seems like a non-entity—a subject void of discussion. Therefore, we look to sports, or government, or business to find a frame of reference...a prototype.

Ethics has been defined as the "idealistic standards of right and wrong"; "specific moral choices made by an individual in his relationship to others." Ethical values have been described as "navigational aids, fixed reference points that keep our human journey from aimless wandering." Webster defines ethics as "the discipline dealing with what is good and bad, and with morality and obligation." During the height of Watergate, Jeb Magruder commented that the reason he found himself in such sorry circumstances was that somewhere along the way he had misplaced his "ethical compass." Voltaire stated, "Men succeed less by their talents than by their character." Our credibility and our ability to influence others are largely determined by the reputation we have built through ethical conduct.

As I pondered the issue of ethics for the music
educator, I looked to the MENC Web site for help, or
at least ideas. I found that the only reference to ethics
was entitled "The Music Code of Ethics." Aha! I found

it! What I found, however, was that this code sets out
guidelines to help music educators and professional musicians avoid
problems stemming from a lack of understanding of each other's role.
It does not address the many other issues that shape ethical behavior
in music performance and in music education. The only other
reference to ethics related to the United States copyright law,
providing legal guidance to music educators. Obviously, there is much
more to ethics for music educators than this.

Many years ago, Adlai Stevenson said, "It is easier to fight for
principles than to live up to them." It is approximately twenty years
ago that Jim Wacker, then coach of the TCU football team and now
deceased, realized that many violations and infractions of the NCAA
rules were occurring in his program. He had the choice of stopping
the infraction by reporting the violations or "riding it out," hoping for
the best. He reported the violations and had to live with the
consequences of the NCAA sanctions that resulted in many losing
seasons and eventually the loss of his job because of the losing record.
When Coach Wacker was asked if his decision was hard, his response
was, "Oh, no, the decision wasn't hard, it was living with the results

206

that was difficult." Today, Jim Wacker is remembered more for his high ethical principles than for his win/loss record as a football coach. He demonstrated ethics of the highest order.

As an advisor to the Honor Commission at Gettysburg College, where I was a professor, I recall that the students found that the most difficult part of following the honor pledge was the responsibility to report an infraction. Reporting a fellow student who was observed cheating was the most difficult part of the code, even though it is a part of the code to which the students pledged. The reluctance was amazing! Ethical behavior not only encompasses the individual but recognition of ethical behavior in others.

None of us were born ethical. We started with nothing...zero ethics and total innocence. Very quickly, that all changed. People 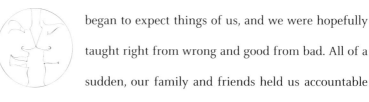 began to expect things of us, and we were hopefully taught right from wrong and good from bad. All of a sudden, our family and friends held us accountable for our behavior, and chances are, we went through some rough times learning what ethics required of us. Hopefully we learned those lessons before we ever knew there was such a word as "ethics."

Essentially, the ethics of music educators or musicians are no different than the ethics of life. They encompass the three basic values that lead to success as human beings:

1. Aspiration

2. Leadership

3. The quest for excellence

To further describe what I mean, it is essential to elaborate on these three basic issues to help bring even perceived success to your life and career.

Aspiration with a good dose of imagination—in short, the entrepreneurial spirit. If you are not willing to risk the unusual, you will have to settle for the ordinary. Yes, failure will occur at times. However, failure will then provide you with a new beginning.

Leadership. The challenge of leadership is to be strong, but not rude. Be kind, but not weak. Be bold, but not bully. Be thoughtful, but not lazy. Be humble, but not timid. Be proud, but not arrogant. Have humor, but without folly. A good objective of leadership is to help those who are doing poorly to do well, and to help those who are doing well to do better. In short, always celebrate the success of others.

208

The quest for excellence. Excellence is not a destination at which one arrives; rather, it is an ideal to which one must aspire, for the job of attaining excellence is one that never ends. I think of excellence as a vicinity, a shifting target that varies from person to person and from ensemble to ensemble by day or by year. Thus, the goal is to get in the vicinity of excellence—and stay there.

Should the execution of these three basic values cause perplexity with your ethical behavior, you must stop and re-evaluate who, what, and where you are with your ethical character. The quest for ethical success must always be present in these three values, for this ethical quest also has no limits. It, too, is an unending quest. To put it in musical terms, every time we experience that dominant seventh chord wanting to resolve to the tonic chord, up comes that submediant chord providing us once again with a deceptive cadence. Thus, that deceptive cadence requires that we continue the ongoing search for the seemingly illusive, perfect, authentic cadence.

Essentially, it is my belief that the bottom line is as follows:

- If something does not feel right, then it probably is not right.
- If you cannot sit down and talk to your family about it at dinner, then do not do it.

- The Golden Rule: "Do unto others as you would have them do unto you." The Talmud states it a little differently: "What is hateful to you, do not do to your fellow man." The principle is universal among mankind. Buddhism says: "Hurt not others in ways that you would find hurtful." Islam says: "Not one of you is a believer until he desires for his brother that which is desired for himself."

Ethical character is built one behavior at a time. Our ability to handle tough choices is vastly improved once we master ordinary ones and become an ethical person by force of habit. Our self-esteem and self-worth must not be measured by how good our performing group is or by our car, house, dress or suit size, golf score, or bank account. It must come through the internal confidence to know right from wrong and good from bad.

The ethics of aspiration, leadership, and excellence embrace the following guidelines:

- Ethics is a code you can live by with comfort.
- Obey the law even though you oppose it.
- Should you ever oppose the law, attempt to change it.
- Do the best thing when there is no right thing.
- Listen to your conscience, but remember that you cannot always trust it.

210

- Talk it out with others, but choose your others carefully.

- Remember that people who matter do not judge and people who judge do not matter.

- Attempt to dispel the thought that "no child left behind" could possibly lead to no school left standing.

- Be prepared to be punished for honesty, aspiration, leadership, and excellence.

- Remember that you will need to pay the price for ethical violation.

- Sweat the small stuff to avoid, if possible, the big stuff.

- Become a cheerleader for ethical champions.

- Permit mistakes; even you make them.

- Mind more than your own business when it comes to ethics.

- Learn to live with shades of gray; life is not all black and white.

- Bear the blame for your behavior.

- Allow your pride to be your guide.

- Don't say what you believe; show what you believe.

- Attempt to be "where the buck stops."

A simple and easy collection of guidelines? No! A necessary collection of guidelines? Absolutely!

Of course, the total picture is not so rosy. Those of us who are substantially engaged in music or any other art form often work in a context where the aspirations and the leadership are misunderstood, or feared, or even opposed. Honesty and excellence simply must overtake all else in these situations, for they are values that speak for themselves. How often do we hear colleagues say what a pleasure it is to be in a situation where everyone understands, and where they do not have to justify their curricular and extra-curricular musical goals? Unfortunately, not very often. When we get enough people who do not accept personal responsibility for excellence and high ethical standards, the program gets the "M" disease—*mediocrity.* Any of our colleagues can be the carriers of this disease.

By the same token, however, our colleagues also carry the cure: the ethics of aspiration, the ethics of leadership, and the ethics of excellence.

I close with the following maxims entitled, "A Statesman's Rules for Daily Conduct." I found this pasted in the cover of the Raessler family Bible, handed down from my great, great grandfather, dated 1882:

> Keep good company or none. Never be idle. If your hands cannot be usefully employed, attend to the cultivation of your mind. Always speak the truth, make few promises. Live up to your engagements. Keep your own secrets, if you have any.

When you speak to a person, look him in the face. Good company and good conversation are the very sinews of virtue. Good character is above all things else. Your character cannot be essentially injured except by your own acts. If anyone speaks ill of you, let your life be so that none will believe him. Ever live, misfortune excepted, within your income. When you retire at night, think about what you have been doing during the day. Say your prayers daily. Make no haste to be rich if you would prosper. Small and steady gains give competency with tranquility of mind. Avoid temptation through fear that you may not withstand it. Earn money before you spend it.

It is no different today. It will be no different tomorrow.

Note: The quotes contained in this chapter have been gathered by Kenneth R. Raessler throughout some fifty years of teaching and extensive lecturing. Kenneth R. Raessler has been a friend and mentor to this author for his entire teaching and conducting career. His advice has always been helpful to me. He has spent his entire professional life helping musicians to be their best. Those who know Ken know the truth in all of this. And for that, all of us who have the privilege of knowing him are deeply grateful. I encourage everyone who reads this book to read Ken's book, *Aspiring to Excel* (GIA, 2003). —JJ

"It is essential that this quest for continued personal growth be ever present..."

"Totem"

Chapter 20

A Code of Ethics from the Inside Out : Thoughts on an Ethical Code for Band Directors

by Richard Floyd

The experience of the context is the true artistic experience and has little to do with the score, as it is not the detail, per se, that places obstacles in the way of understanding.

Professional ethics of a conductor is not technical ability, but a spiritual attitude.

The real problem of our time is how to reunite technique with context. There is another technique of which today's world is no longer aware, which is infinitely more difficult. The difference between these two concepts of technique contains everything of any importance that today's world should and does not know.

216

Expression marks, whether sparse and schematic, as in Bach, or abundant and realistically minute as with our contemporaries are not of the slightest use if the sense and the spirit of the music are not captured.

Wilhelm Furtwangler

The dictionary defines the word "code" as a system of accepted laws and regulations that govern procedures or behavior in particular circumstances or within a particular profession. Looking further, one finds the meaning of the word "ethics" described as a system of moral principles governing the appropriate conduct for an individual or group. Pretty dry stuff. But taken together, these definitions give us a general but generic expectation of what is commonly referred to as a "professional code of ethics."

Such codes exist all around us. Doctors have them. Attorneys have them. Politicians even have them! If you think about it, virtually all professions and trades have a code of ethics in one form or another. They are intended as guideposts for how members of a profession treat one another and those they serve. Good idea!

But contemplate for a minute what essential elements should be included in a code of ethics uniquely forged for band conductors.

Certainly the obligatory "Thou shalts" and "Thou shalt nots" would be present. References to integrity, high ideals, and dedication are fundamental. Appropriate interaction with students would be high on the list.

But we are members of a unique breed. First, we are involved in a compelling art that in and of itself can be a powerful mistress. At the same time, we are intertwined with diverse publics including, but not limited to, colleagues, students, parents, administrators, and others in the music and educational community—any one of which can consume us. So how do we balance our moral and ethical obligations to such a plethora of professional, social, and personal entities?

The simple answer might be to stir up the alphabet soup of professional organizations that surround us. Certainly the collective wisdom of NBA, ABA, CBDNA, ASBDA (and the list goes on and on) combined with countless state organizations and the global vision of MENC have acted to provide a clear path for us to follow. A quick Internet search reveals countless references to "conduct codes" for music educators. Many are comprehensive in nature, others are more tightly focused, and virtually all are well meaning.

Such external guidance is all well and good, but is it sufficient? And more important, should it be the primary force that sculpts our behavior? We often tell students that only after they have mastered a

218 piece of music inside and out and have come to terms with their personal feelings about it can they truly make a judgment about its relative merit. This precept can easily be applied to our quest for our own professional principles. Perhaps we should take ownership of our own ethics and look inward to find the guiding forces that mold who we are as members of our chosen profession.

Surely the mantle of ethics for a musician, conductor, and teacher would be more meaningful if it did not stem from some external code of conduct, but rather from a blueprint for behavior based on an internal perspective of who we are and what we stand for. Such a code would embrace our fundamental attitudes towards:

- Passion and reverence for our art

- Love for our students

- Respect for our colleagues

- A personal perspective of our own self-worth

Interestingly, many existing codes address students, colleagues, and the public at large, but reference to the art we strive to serve is rare or nonexistent. Very strange. How can we begin a discussion on how to conduct ourselves professionally without homage to the central core of our focus? Surely an affirmation of our belief in the art of music must be the basis for how we conduct ourselves.

In the band world, it is very easy to become immersed in the peripheral activities of administration, recruitment, fund-raising, grading, travel, public relations, competition, etc., to the extent that we lose sight of what must be the central focus of all we do. Frederick Fennel often stated, "The truth is in the score." His passionate challenge to band conductors remains timeless. Simply put, all decisions and actions must be based on the pure essence of the music as created by the composer. Surely that mantra can be expanded to serve as a guiding beacon for all that we do professionally, personally, and ethically.

Perhaps the first and most important ethical challenge we face each day as we embrace the countless responsibilities that confront us is to uphold music as the centerpiece of all that we do. It is so easy to focus on such external factors as building a band program, achieving competitive success (more on that later), and musical "one-upmanship." In so doing, we quickly lose site of the primary reason for our existence as band directors and music educators—which is to create and share deeply meaningful musical experiences with the students we are privileged to teach.

Unfortunately, it is possible to achieve a high mark of band director success with minimal musical focus. Many recognized band programs are measured in terms of extrinsic markers, such as trophies, travel, and other highly visible endeavors. Such activities are

220

certainly not inherently evil and can be a by-product of an infinitely successful program, but when they become the primary focus of a program, the true quintessence of our reason for being is lost.

On the other hand, it is noteworthy to observe that the most successful and highly respected members of our profession always seem to have their musical center. Their every action and deed appears to exist to achieve the realization of musical truth for themselves and their students. In so doing, the non-musical and sometimes tangential elements of the profession are consistently met and addressed, but they never supplant music making as the focal point of daily endeavors. Arguably, acting with such musical passion and reverence could be construed as the highest form of professional, ethical conduct for a member of our proud profession.

Now, what about our students? In one fashion or another, we are all teachers. Whether in a beginning band classroom or before the most sophisticated college wind ensemble, our focus remains on the musical lives of the young people who are in our charge. Universally, the expectation is that we kindle, guide, and develop the musical potential of each of our students while at the same time encouraging them to embark on a lifelong voyage of musical enrichment. These responsibilities to our students are fundamental. But there is more.

Remember that, in general, students come to us by choice, filled with curiosity and enthusiasm. It is our moral responsibility to be the guardian of these qualities as we nurture the zest students hold for learning an instrument and making music. This makes perfectly good sense, so why the concern? Because we as band directors are traditionally driven by the passion and enthusiasm we hold for the art we serve. While music in general and band in particular can be the center of our personal universe, we must remember that our students and their families have diverse educational priorities and personal interests.

We must be cognizant of the fact that we represent only one small part of the total educational process. Thus, it is imperative that we remain sensitive to each student's needs in terms of academic pursuits, family life, and extracurricular activities. We have a moral responsibility to design and implement instructional strategies that provide a high level of educational and musical experiences while recognizing the complex academic, family, and social commitments of our students. To that end, it is essential that we maintain a reasonable and proper balance of pre-school and out-of-school rehearsal and performance schedules. If we do not maintain this balance, then we risk extinguishing the very flame of musical excitement that initially attracted students to our programs.

222   Our peers must also be a key component of our ethical framework. It is generally acknowledged that the "world of bands" tends to be closely knit. While our days are filled with student interaction, we are also surrounded by a musical community comprised of other directors, administrators, composers, and a profusion of music-related professionals. Since music is such a communal experience, we share our lives daily with kindred spirits. As with students, there are fundamental attitudes that must prevail. We must remain professional, act with integrity, and contribute in a meaningful way to the educational community in which we live and work.

With that said, there is both good news and bad news regarding our relationships with colleagues. The good news is the fact that, by nature, band directors tend to be sharing and caring. There is willingness in the profession to be supportive of one another and to offer assistance whenever asked. This is a laudable trait and one that we as a profession should nurture and protect. The bad news is the reality that competitive activities and ego involvement can easily erode this prized quality. While certain strata of our profession foster competition in a number of guises, we as a profession must monitor our attitude regarding competition and curb any temptation to allow competitive advantage or our own ego to supersede our commitment to one another and the students we collectively serve. Thus, the twin nemeses of competitive success and musical one-upmanship mentioned earlier must be avoided at all costs.

So how does our own self-worth as human beings factor into all of this? After all, we tend to think of ethics in terms of our interaction with others. This is true, but certainly what we have to offer to our art and what we bring to the table in our dealings with others is directly related to our intellectual resources, social attitudes, and our personal quest for continued growth. We have an obligation to all in our professional world to be the best musicians and teachers we can be and to constantly challenge ourselves to seek musical and personal growth. To do anything less diminishes our effectiveness as a member of our proud profession.

In a radio interview on his eightieth birthday, Bruno Walter was asked what he had to look forward to since he had already collaborated with all of the great orchestras and musical artists of his day. His response was that he hoped to go on growing and learning. Similarly, Sir George Solti noted near the end of his life that the more he studied, the more he realized he needed to learn to become the musician that he wanted to be. It is essential that this quest for continued personal growth be ever present in our lives.

Equally important, our thirst for the acquisition of knowledge and personal development must be larger than the "world of bands" that surrounds us. We must prompt our musical curiosity to explore a broader horizon of musical thought and artistic expression than the narrow confines of our daily existence. We owe it to ourselves and to our students to avoid becoming complacent and simply focusing on the project at hand and the pedagogical skills required for immediate mastery. The greater the breadth and depth we seek in our own musicianship, the more meaningful and global the experiences we have to share with our students become.

Thus, such a blueprint for ethics requires more than simply observing a code or following the rules. It demands that each of us examine our personal passion for music, our commitment to students, our attitudes towards others in the profession, and an inward appraisal of our own self-worth. The net outcome should be a unique, personal code of ethics that embraces the unique dimensions of each individual and the richness of the musical and educational world in which we function.

A long-time mentor told a story of a gentleman who got in a taxi and requested to be transported to a certain destination. Upon arrival, the passenger asked the driver the amount of the fare and carefully doled out the exact change sans any tip. The driver took the payment and counted it carefully. Seeing a look of puzzlement on the driver's face, the passenger asked if the amount was correct, to which the driver responded, "Yes, sir, it is correct but that sure don't make it right."

As a member of the proud profession of band conductors, it   **225**

should not be enough to simply go by the book and make it correct.

We must have the vision, desire, and commitment to look deeply

within ourselves and make it right. Our art, our students, our

colleagues, and indeed ourselves deserve no less.

Section Three

The Resting Place

"The time has come to acknowledge the root of our ethical dilemma.

"Stupa Steeple"

Chapter 21

One Body, Two Selves

Among other findings, Davidson's work has shown that meditators can regulate their cerebral activity, yielding more focus and composure. By contrast, most untrained subjects asked to focus on an object cannot limit their mental activity to a single task. The monks who had practiced the longest showed the greatest brain changes, leading Davidson to think that they may have effected permanent changes. His most intriguing results have come from observing advanced practitioners meditating on compassion. The brain changes observed during this practice seem to show that intensively generating goodwill produces indicators of an extreme state of well-being. While the sources of all kinds of disorders and dysfunctions have been studied extensively, there is almost no literature on what those scientists sometimes call "healing emotion." (p. 40)

Barry Boyce

"Two Sciences of the Mind"

Shambhala Sun, November 2005

230

Pondering such split-brain cases, some scientists and philosophers have raised a disquieting possibility: perhaps each of us really consists of two minds running in harness. In an intact brain, of course, the corpus callosum acts as a constant two-way internal communications channel between two hemispheres. So our everyday behavior does not betray the existence of two streams of consciousness flowing along within our skulls. It may be, the philosopher Thomas Nagel has written, that "the ordinary, simple idea of a single person will come to seem quaint some day, when the complexities of the human control system become clearer and we become less certain that there is anything very important that we are *one* of."

It is sobering to reflect how ignorant humans have been about the workings of their own brains for most of our history. Aristotle, after all, thought the point of the brain was to cool the blood. The more that breakthroughs like the recent one in brain-scanning open up the mind to scientific scrutiny, the more we may be pressed to give up the comforting metaphysical ideas like interiority, subjectivity and the soul. Let's enjoy them while we can. (p. 13)

Jim Holt
"Of Two Minds"

New York Times Magazine

M a y   2 0 0 5

Although some authorities have been reluctant to credit the disconnected minor hemisphere even with being conscious, it is our own interpretation based on a large number and variety of nonverbal tests, that the minor hemisphere is indeed a conscious system in its own right, perceiving, thinking, remembering, reasoning, willing and emoting, all at a characteristically human level, and that both the left and the right hemisphere may be conscious simultaneously in different, even in mutually conflicting, mental experiences that run along in parallel. (p. 292)

The single most dramatic finding from these investigations is that the ability to speak, and to a lesser extent to comprehend language, is limited to one, the *dominant,* hemisphere. In more than nine out of ten patients it is the left cortical hemisphere that speaks, communicates through writing, and deals with other aspects of language with ease. The right hemisphere has only limited language comprehension and can't talk (although it can sing). When a split-brain patient talks, it is his or her dominant hemisphere that is in control. The nondominant hemisphere is mute. It can still signal, however, by nodding the head or making meaningful signs with the fingers of the opposite hand. (p. 290)

Christof Koch

The Quest for Consciousness

While I am not a psychiatrist or a neurologist (that work should be left to those more qualified than I), I have made some observations for musicians to ponder. It seems to me that, given recent brain scan research, which shows that the two halves of our brains share an internal communication channel (the corpus callosum), it may be time for musicians and artists to recognize and accept that we are indeed two brain selves in one body. We might also want to entertain

232 the fact that we get into ethical and musical predicaments when we shuttle abruptly between these two very different worlds. Loving treatment of our colleagues (and ourselves) and those who play and sing for us might be easier than we have previously thought. What is necessary, however, is that we devote some thought to the subject.

Let me surmise a situation or two using these recent brain theories. First, it has been recognized through neurological research that it is possible for the brain to change shape. That is, with protracted activity, accessed portions of the brain enlarge while others diminish in size. I recently had a student who I admire greatly for her intellectual zest challenge the central idea I presented in *The Musician's Soul*: that meditation is a prerequisite to music making because it allows one to access silence. My student argued that she does not enjoy meditation because "I enjoy thinking." She also commented that meditation seemed to be a wasted activity because she could not see the value in thinking about nothing. She likes to think—it is exciting; meditation is boring.

Yet this student struggles as a musician because she is told she cannot connect with sound, and she views herself as amusical. I believe the answer to her issue and all of our issues may lie in accepting the fact that as artists, we have two brains to contend with, which must be developed separately if we are to be any success at what we do: both as humans and as musicians. Such a radical statement has profound implications for the training of artists and musicians.

233

Earlier in this book, I wrote about two aspects of Weston Noble's life: journaling and picking up trash. Both of these activities are centered in the part of the brain that meditates and also makes music. According to the research, decades of such activity cause the brain to change shape which, in Weston's case, has an impact indirectly (and directly) upon his music making, whether or not he is willing to acknowledge it. It seems to me now that the mimetical principles I espoused in *The Musician's Soul* have scientific merit. If one continues to practice both some type of meditation and mimetics as one rehearses, then one is slowly, over a long period of time, altering the shape and function of one of the "brains." Weston has retired after fifty-seven years of employing these practices. There is no doubt in my mind that a lifetime of contemplation has reshaped this man's mind (and spirit) so the music he conducts is a direct by-product of this neurological reshaping.

On the opposite side of this equation, I know musicians who simply are unable to carry humane, caring (and ethical) behaviors outside the rehearsal room. These persons are schizophrenic in an artistic sense in that they do not want or need to stay in the "self" wherein creativity and beauty dwell. They are there for music making only, and they immediately move to their other self when dealing with people. These persons believe that their "one brain" holds all the answers, and they retreat to the cognitive side. It is clear that these persons simply have not spent enough time with themselves to change the shape of their brain. They continue to use the same brain they had at childhood, with all its insecurities, shallowness, and self-centered characteristics.

So what answers does all of this hold? If we are willing to embrace scientific research and follow its lead, it may hold many answers to an artist's ethical dilemma. As I examine the lives of great musicians, I am now becoming increasingly convinced that part of their "gift" was an intuitive sense that they were indeed one self with two "brains." Picasso's bizarre life behaviors had nothing to do with his creative being; they seemed to happily coexist much to the exasperation of those around him. Paul Hindemith was not the most pleasant of human beings, but his music seems to live in totally different worlds than his lived life. Stravinsky was edgy and pointed, but his music had another life beyond his human interactions. If one ponders the brilliant career of Robert Shaw, many painstaking hours were spent in both score study and writing letters to his choir. Throughout Shaw's career, I am certain these activities "reshaped" the portion of his brain that brought a unique human voice to his musicianship—and those of us who experienced Shaw know he did not like to be jolted out of that brain! Frederick Fennell's music making was kilned through a life of thought and reflection about music. It seems that, in some way, he knew of these two "brains" and worked to develop the artistic brain over the other "default" brain, the one that is prone to rash behaviors and inhumane paths.

When I was a graduate student at Temple University, I was Elaine

Brown's graduate assistant, so it fell upon me to pick up Eugene
Ormandy at his residence at the Barclay Hotel in Philadelphia. I have
many Ormandy stories, but this one has caused me to wonder over
the years; and now I think I have an answer. I had picked up Maestro
Ormandy for a piano rehearsal of the Beethoven *Choral Fantasy,*
which was being held on the main campus of Temple University. As I
drove up Broad Street, Maestro Ormandy (who by this time knew I
was a conducting student of "Missus Brown") for some reason began
a discussion with me on *Elijah.* He peppered me with questions and
started to talk about some "ideas" he had about the piece. He talked
and talked and talked. As I turned off Broad Street, he had me so
enthralled and distracted that I almost hit a pedestrian. The
pedestrian kicked the rear of the car repeatedly. The noise was
unbelievable. But Ormandy kept talking about Mendelssohn! For a
second, he broke sentence and told me to "keep driving, Mendelssohn
is more important." I was a bit shaken at the pounding and denting
my car had just taken. But Ormandy stayed with Mendelssohn—even
all the way home. In fact, when he entered into the piano rehearsal
(for those who knew Ormandy, his photographic memory was
legend), he looked at the choir, and before starting, he motioned to Dr.
Brown. I heard him ask Dr. Brown, "What piece are we
doing, Mendelssohn?" She said, *"Beethoven Choral Fantasy."* "Ah,
yes." And we took off into the piece like a bolt in Ormandy style. I am

not sure Ormandy ever left that side of his brain during the pedestrian attack!

Our ability to lead a creative, ethical, and happy life appears to be directly proportional to the time we spend reshaping half of our brain to increase its domination over both our music making and ourselves. Mistakes in behavior are inevitable when the corpus callosum functions as an informational superhighway that confuses us into believing that we are one-brained creatures. We make artistic decisions based upon emotion and ego, not upon that portion of the brain where love and music reside. It is a human battle for music educators, conductors, and performers to be comfortable with that other brain—staying there when dealing with musical matters and going there when dealing with things musical.

One body, two selves—I believe it is true and has been true for those who are willing to accept this unsettling fact. Perhaps the time has come to acknowledge that the root of our ethical dilemma rests in the accurate perception of our true functioning. It is both an artist's blessing and a curse. To acknowledge this level of complexity is to begin the hard work of using both sides of our two selves—not as a sickness, but as a great gift.

"Ethics must be born of careful and deliberate forethought."

"A View Through"

Chapter 22

Some Guidelines and Further Definitions: An Ethical Code for Musicians

The rehearsal or music classroom must be a kind of home that offers its inhabitants a sense of belonging, of individuality strengthened by expectation, of security born out of mutual respect. The musician should feel known but revered; the conductor or teacher, exposed but esteemed. Reason for excellence need not preclude acceptance of human foibles; neither should devotion and understanding be devoid of rigor. Care is by nature compensatory, seeking to provide that which otherwise is lacking.

The habit of reflection is the ideal trait of the educated mind, taking for its concern what others may be satisfied to take for granted. Education should foster this habit, should teach patience in the understanding and construction of ideas. But it should also teach us to consider feelings, to anticipate the probable effect of our actions

240 and words on others, and to temper these when they augur injury. Education is this forethought rather than afterthought, abiding thought rather than sporadic thought.

adapted and paraphrased from the philosophy of
the Brookline, Massachusetts High School
In Search of Excellence

We need to recall the angel aspect of the word, recognizing words as independent carriers of soul between people. We need to recall that we do not just make up words or learn them in school, or fully ever have them under control. Words, like angels, are powers which have invisible powers over us. They are personal presences which have whole mythologies, genders, genealogies, histories and vogues; and their own guarding, blaspheming, creating and annihilating effects. For words are persons. This aspect of the word transcends their nominalistic definitions and contexts and evokes in our souls a universal resonance. Without the inherence of soul in words, speech would not move us, words would not provide forms for carrying our lives and giving sense to our deaths. (p. 9)

James Hillman
Re-Visioning Psychology

He who knows nothing, loves nothing. He who can do nothing, understands nothing. He who understands nothing is worthless. But he who understands also loves, notices, sees.... The more knowledge is inherent in a thing, the greater the love.... Anyone who imagines that all fruits ripen at the same time as the strawberries knows nothing about grapes.

Paracelsus

When does one ever know a human being? Perhaps only after one has realized the impossibility of knowledge and renounced the desire for it and finally ceased to feel even the need of it. But then what one achieves is no longer knowledge, it is simply a kind of co-existence; and this too is one of the guises of love.

Iris Murdoch
_____
Under the Net

Love is the active concern for the life and the growth of that which we love. (p. 25)

Erich Fromm
_____
The Art of Loving

Peak few words, but say them with quietude and sincerity,
And they will be long lasting,
For a raging wind cannot blow all morning,
Nor a sudden rainstorm last throughout the day.

Why is this so?
Because it is the nature of the sky and earth to be frugal.
Even human beings cannot alter this nature
Without suffering the consequences.

When we sincerely follow the ethical path,
We become one with it.
When we become one with the ethical path, it embraces us.
When we completely lose our way, we become one with loss.
When we become one with loss, loss embraces us.

242

When we sincerely follow the great integrity,

We become one with it.

When we are one with great integrity,

We become one with it.

When we are one with great integrity, it embraces us.

But when nothing is done sincerely,

Nothing and no one embraces us.

Ralph Alan Dale
Tao Te Ching (new translation of Lao Tzu)

In the following pages I offer nothing more than simple facts. Plain arguments and common sense, and have no other preliminaries to settle with the reader, other than that he will divest himself of prejudice and prepossession, and suffer his reason and his feelings to determine for themselves; that he will put on, or rather that he will not put off, the true character of a man, and generously enlarge his views beyond the present day.

Thomas Paine
Common Sense

My image of ethics is rather different. My image would be of a table with many legs. We all know that a table with many legs wobbles when the floor on which it stands is not even, but even such a table is very hard to turn over and that is how I see ethics: as a table with many legs, which wobbles a lot, but is very hard to turn over. (p. 28)

Hilary Putnam
Ethics Without Ontology

Ethos, from which we get the word *ethics,* 243
originally meant a place where animals
frequent. When we herd together, how do we
behave? Do we look after one another? Do we
take care of the place where we gather—the
land, the city, the drinking water? Are we
welcome here? Can we be ourselves? These are basic questions of
human existence, and how we answer them and live them has
everything to do with our ethics. (p. 214)

Ethics is a way of recognizing that although we are each alone in this
universe, we are all alone together. We can make a good life not only
by protecting each other but by being creative together and taking our
pleasures from one another. (pp. 215–216)

Ethics is a form of soul care because it clears away significant
obstacles to the movement of life. Conversely, failure in ethics is
always a signal of some fundamental anxiety or blind spot about the
nature of things. Any effort toward living ethically is a way of caring
for the soul, and anyone seriously interested in living a spiritual life
might first consider, honestly and deeply, the state of his ethics and
the positive call of his conscience. (p. 220)

Thomas Moore

The Soul's Religion

𝓑y this point you may have pondered several viewpoints on what

an ethical code might be or how it might be shaped. Shaping of such

a code is certainly influenced by one's surroundings and the nature of

the life business that is being carried on in the midst of such

244

behavior, whether it be a rehearsal, a classroom, a church, a school, or a university. We have taken a look at two musicians whose approach to everyday life and teaching is colored by how they choose to partial out the aspects of their daily life. However, there are some commonalities that seem to be appearing, which could direct our reflection and the direction of our walk.

It should now be clear that we are dealing with behavior within and among a group of human beings who are making music. I would like to revisit the Thomas Moore quote above, because that quote begins to bring clarity to a very murky domain for all of us. Consider the various definitions of the word "herd." Pay particular attention to those definitions I have highlighted.

herd *n*
1. a large number of domestic animals, especially cattle, often of the same breed, that are kept, driven, or reared together **2.** a large number of wild animals of the same kind that live, feed, and travel as a group   **3. a large group of people, often with a common interest, purpose, or bond 4. ordinary people, considered as acting or thinking as a group and lacking the ability to think as individuals**
herd *v*
1. *vt* to drive, keep, or look after domestic animals as a group
2. *vt* to move people or animals somewhere as a group, or collect them into a group **3.** *vi* to gather together or go somewhere as a group

245

Considering the above definitions in combination with Thomas Moore's quote, a working definition of ethics should certainly deal with how we behave when we are in a group—in this case, musicians. Whether those musicians are our ensembles, colleagues, or others we encounter in our professional journey, our way of behaving in this context has everything to do with what ethics should be. Clear ethical thought and a clear ethical pathway is necessary on the musician's walk because how we behave will always impact our music making.

It might be helpful to remove us from examining human interactions and turn to the animal world for an ethical model. I live in Yardley, Pennsylvania. Yardley is unique because in addition to being a community of human beings, it serves as a peaceful cohabitat for humans and many ducks, geese, and several genetic aberrations that fill in that portion of the bird kingdom.

There is a beautiful lake in the center of Yardley, which indirectly feeds a canal that passes through the community. My home sits on the bank of the Delaware Canal, which is also the thoroughfare for the town's many ducks, geese, and swimming fowl that navigate from one end of town to the other, moving from lake, to canal, and sometimes strolling the streets.

There are a considerable number of these creatures in town. As many as several hundred, I suppose, although one always sees from twenty-five to fifty "herded" together in a gaggle going about their

246   daily business. You never see one walking alone. They always travel in groups, most of the time in very large groups. They are capable of calm, quiet beauty, as well as the most irritating noises known to humankind. I watch them as I go about my daily business. At exactly 6:30 each morning, they gather across the canal at a neighbor's house in a large gaggle (perhaps one hundred of them), and they come out of the canal and stand quietly. They politely and quietly wait for the resident of that house to come out. They wait for approximately three minutes, and if no one appears, they begin to make noise that is deafening. They continue the attention-getting noise until the residents appear with their morning food: bags of bread. When the residents appear, they immediately stop the quacking, eat their food, and turn around and get into the canal.

At approximately 7:10 each morning, they swim about a half block, exit the canal, and walk northward on the street, defying traffic. They are heading to house number two for more food! It is fascinating to watch their movement. There are no geese or ducks left behind. They travel in one tight group. It is an unusual group, too, because it is not only ducks of all colors and varieties, but black Canadian geese, white geese, and another variety of genetic recombination that looks like a goose with a rooster's head. They clearly are not ducks, but they walk in the midst of the others. As they move down the street, you can see two one-footed ducks. These

247

handicapped creatures do not bring up the back of the gaggle but, instead, are kept at the center of the group toward the front, surrounded by others. Because they hop to "walk," they move slower, so the others move at their pace. Occasionally, you might see them lose balance a bit, but two ducks mysteriously appear to keep their friends upright! They appear at house number two, and stand in a group again, silently, until they feel their routine is being disrupted. Then they begin the ear-shattering cackle, bringing resident two outside with food. She feeds them near her homemade "Duck crossing" sign.

Later in the day, you can usually sight all of them again in the town's lake adjacent to Starbucks. They swim co-mingled, sharing the same food and water space. For some reason, children are always greeted with a quack!

Now let's apply this bit of nature to musicians. Rarely, if ever, do you see musicians in groups. If musicians do travel in small groups, "lesser" musicians or "musically handicapped" musicians are usually not in the group. Even at conventions, musicians seem not to herd particularly well. They usually travel alone. Wouldn't it be wonderful if musicians behaved like the Yardley fowl subculture? Those musicians would take pleasure from being together. They would move together in a group, where all are viewed as equals—even those who might need more care, like the one-footed ducks. All of the feathered fowl share and, at least on the surface, show compassion for those among them who look different and who may have less.

I sit on the bench across from my house and wonder (admittedly, a bit foolishly) whether this group has an ethical code. By definition, they must. They know how to be together. They look after one another. They seem to welcome each other. They also seem to be able to be themselves as they move through their daily business! Could musicians, performers, and music educators pass the simple litmus test I just put to the gaggle of Yardley geese? Probably not. We have problems being with ourselves, let alone knowing the right way to behave in a group of us. In fact, bad behavior seems to make itself known when we group or herd. Why? Because we probably haven't appropriated enough time either in our personal world or in our professional education to formulate such a "code" of behavior. To parallel the stunning statement from the Brookline Schools, which is both a philosophy of teaching and an ethical code, perhaps clarifies a possible direction and the beginning of construction of an ethical code.

Always consider the feelings of others, and anticipate and predict the effect of all of your actions and words, no matter how small, on others. Temper both thoughts and words when they might damage the spirit. Ethics, in its truest sense, is the way in which we choose to be with each other in our musical world. Ethics must be born of careful   and   deliberate   forethought   rather   than   impulsive afterthought, and ethics must occupy our abiding thoughts each day

of our lives.

We must begin to herd better. Great music assumes we will herd well together so our combined voice is more powerful than any one sound. Without that "community" of "I and thou," as Martin Buber says, music loses its strength and potency to fire and inspire the human spirit in the classroom, rehearsal room, and performance hall.

What follows is my meager attempt to begin dialogue and thought concerning an "ethical code" for musicians. I do not propose to hold the magical semantic key to the way we should think and act as musicians. But I do know that each one of us should have some path to follow, some way to keep perspective within us when our love of music seems to empower us to be inhumane in varying degrees to those around us. While music can provide a beacon in times of both community and personal need, be careful and mindful that it is easy to allow ego to interfere with good judgment and compassionate behavior. Music cannot be the defense of inhumane and, at times, irrational or condescending behavior toward others.

Also remember that as artists in this complex world, we possess a powerful tool for loving and caring in the most compassionate ways for others. Music, as we all know, can speak more directly to one's spirit and one's soul than spoken language can. Great art and poetry also possess equal power over the human spirit. Strive to understand the power of our gift to improve the lives of others, including our-selves, and the profound and long-lasting effects of our actions upon the feelings and the very souls we are entrusted with each time we enter a music classroom or rehearsal.

I think a list of ethical "standards" deserves pondering in one's silent moments. Amend and add to this list as your experience has taught you.

1. Strive for awareness of the world while you make music.
2. Be grateful to everyone.
3. Foster reflection. Consider feelings, anticipate the probable effect of our actions and words upon others, and temper those when they augur injury. Music making should be forethought rather than afterthought, abiding thought rather than sporadic thought.*
4. Through your music, practice only good things.
5. Teach compassion and love in all things.
6. Hold a mirror to your soul daily.
7. Do not use music to hide from life and its complexities; allow music to provide strength and insight for living.
8. Teach life, not just music.
9. Guard against arrogance when fearful.
10. Seek silence and solitude when chaos, musical or otherwise, ensues.
11. Make an effort daily to transform your thinking from what you have experienced to what you know is right.
12 Follow your instincts for what is right.
13. See only the good in all rehearsals.
14. Accept the music of ensembles as a personal gift.
15. Visit the joyful times in your life frequently.
16. Never use words when making music that hurt or demean the spirits of others.

17. Maintain your vulnerability and love when musicians hurt you.

18. Respect and marvel in age and experience.

19. Learn from experienced and older colleagues.

20. Live and teach compassionately. Work hard every day to understand compassion.

21. Be humble concerning your musical gifts.

22. In your teaching, daily try to make yourself less so others become more.

23. Write nothing to another colleague or musician. Always discuss issues face to face.

24 Allow one week to pass before acting on a situation with others arising out of music making.

25. Revel in the gifts of others.

26. Never speak ill of others or hurt others using "music" or "art" as your reason for doing so.

27. Be not fearful about what you do not know.

28. Love yourself, then others.

29. Apologize when you have hurt others; then move on.

30. Seek advice often, especially in times of confusion or fear.

31. Be patient with others who struggle with what you do easily.

32. Let other musicians find their own musical way. Respect the musical opinions and ideas of others.

33. Create awe and wonder at every musical turn.

34. Share music often with everyone.

35. Let others make music with you.

36. Love and be patient with those who are not musicians.

37. Argue not about religion.

38. Conduct classes and rehearsals as life apprenticeships in their ideal form; music and life that is devoted to inquiry, touched by beauty, informed by justice, guided by reason, girded by simplicity, and graced by elegance. Through music, we will learn what it means to live well.

* Paraphrased from the Educational Philosophy of Brookline High School (Brookline, MA).

Being human is a most precarious condition. It is not a substance but a presence, a whisper calling in the wilderness. Man is hard of inner hearing, but he has sharp, avid eyes. The power he unlocks surpasses the power that he is, dazzling him. He has a capacity for extravagance, sumptuousness, presumption. His power is explosive. Human being is boundless, but being human has a respect for bounds. The human situation may be characterized as a polarity of human being and being human. (p. 100)

Abraham Joshua Heschel
Who Is Man?

When one is new to this profession, daily pondering is recommended. Repetitive pondering breeds habitual thought patterns. Key to the effectiveness of any such "code" is the ability to revisit it and to see the wisdom in its words.

While the list above is numeric, all points are important. There is no hierarchy in this list, just continual pondering over the entire list. What I believe such lists have always done is to both create and sharpen life awarenesses. One should strive to be in a state of constant awareness about one's relationships in music. It is not a specific code of ethics that will multiply the joy in your professional life but rather the awareness that is born out of a newfound reality. Problems ensue when unawareness is present. Hurt is always created in states of unawareness. Unawareness is the "enemy." When unawareness is present, music will suffer. A nonverbal communication begins to overpower the language of music so the voice of music is lessened or

silenced.

I suppose for any Code of Ethics to be successful, there must be a policing "body"—a panel (or some such vehicle) that will dole out punishment to offenders. May I propose that the policing body be each of our own souls? No panels, no executive committees. Just ourselves. Isn't that ultimately how we judge our music making, at least when we are alone and in our most silent places? Monitor your own walk, my friends. Then we can experience the true rewards of awareness and the humanity that is music's gift.

"...we cannot lead where we have not been."

Photo by Br. Emmanuel Morinelli, O.C.S.O.

Chapter 23

Nonmusical Considerations for the Church Musician

by James Abbington

One thing has suddenly hit me—that nothing counts except love and that a solitude that is not simply the wide-openness of love and freedom is nothing. Love and solitude are the one ground of true maturity and freedom...true solitude embraces everything, for it is the fullness of love that rejects nothing and no one, is open all in all. (cover page)

Thomas Merton
Learning to Love

256

*I*n 1988, C. Harry Causey published a book entitled *Things They Didn't Tell Me About Being a Minister of Music* (Music Revelation, 1988). This book takes a humorous look at some serious topics every church musician needs to understand. The chapters are entitled:

"They Didn't Tell Me I Would Have to Be a Politician"

"...Married to the Job"

"...a Financial Wizard"

"...a Psychologist"

"...a Producer"

"...a Bible Scholar"

"...a Servant"

"...an Administrator"

"...a Personality"

"...a Disciplinarian"

At the time this book was published, there were few, if any, resources that focused on the nonmusical attributes of music leadership in the church. Causey's writing was witty, practical, inspirational, and challenging to me as a young minister of music at a very large urban congregation in Detroit.

In 1994, Robin Knowles Wallace wrote a similar book expanding on Causey's position entitled *Things They Never Tell You Before You Say "Yes"* (Abingdon Press, 1994).

As a music minister, I quickly discovered there were many nonmusical considerations, duties, responsibilities, and unspoken expectations that went above and beyond my musical preparation and training. For example, it was one thing to identify members of the choir as either soprano, alto, tenor, or bass, but it was another thing to know their names and be able to address them as individuals.

The first and foremost requirement of a church musician is to love the Lord God with all one's heart and mind. If musicians do not first love God and the people of God, then all their talents, skills, and training will not help them to succeed.[1] Although this seems basic and simple, musicians often talk church talk but refuse to walk church walk. Just as ministers are called of God, so, too, church musicians are called of God. There is a major distinction between a *musician who works in a church* and a *church musician.*

James Robert Davidson defines a minister of music as "the person who combines the tasks of ministry and music leadership...and is often ordained to the ministry with music as the tool of his  [or her] calling. This role includes the gathering of the people, the teaching of them, and the caring for them through a musical dimension within the total redemptive-creativity activity." He explains that the term "is relatively recent to church music having appeared around the mid-twentieth century among evangelical Protestant churches in America. A real impetus toward its use came from the Southern Baptist Convention with its establishment of the Department of Church Music (1941) as a part of the Sunday School Board and its implementation of Schools of Church Music in the various seminaries." An even more important difference, says Davidson, is that

> unlike the director of music, the minister of music is involved with more than simply choral and instrumental ensembles and leading the congregational singing. He [or she] is concerned with the total congregation, what the needs are of the congregation as individuals, and what music will best meet the needs, and effect a desired response. Through his [or her] choice and use of music, he [or she] is involved in the process of instilling theological concepts as well as a devotional vocabulary. His [or her] ability to know his [or her] congregation and individual attitudes, to identify with these, and to provide the catalyst for a feeling of community in the proclamation of Christian truth through music compromise the discipline and limits of his [or her] work.[2]

Although this definition does not reflect what many ministers of music do, it is certainly a Herculean model to which we can all aspire.

This chapter will focus on nonmusical issues and considerations for the church choir director, many of which violate simple and basic moral, ethical, spiritual, and professional conduct. Topics range from illegally photocopying music; to criticizing, disrobing, and dismantling the musical work of other choirs and their directors; to refusing to work with pastors and other ministerial staff associated with worship leadership.

photocopying music

Almost without fail, the first page of every copy of music has a copyright date and a statement such as: "Photocopying of this publication without permission of the publisher is a violation of the U.S. Code of Law for which the responsible individual or institution is subject to criminal prosecution. No one is exempt," or other similar language. A complete copy of the United States Copyright Law and further information regarding the copyright law may be obtained online at the U.S. Copyright Office Web site (www.copyright.gov), or by writing The U.S. Copyright Office, Library of Congress, Washington, DC 20559.

It is important to know that you can request permission to make photocopies of copyrighted music by securing licenses from the copyright owner prior to making any of the copies. You can also obtain permission to use many congregationally sung compositions by contacting the applicable licensing agency, such as OneLicense.net.

260

They can be reached at www.onelicense.net, by calling (800) 663-1501, or by writing 7343 S. Mason Avenue, Chicago, IL 60638. Another such licensing agency is Christian Copyright Licensing, Inc. (CCLI), www.ccli.com. It is important to know that a reprint license *does not* grant the right to photocopy or duplicate any choral music, cantatas, musicals, handbell music, keyboard arrangements, vocal solos, or instrumental works. The license grants duplicating rights for congregational music only.

The law provides for the owner of a copyright to recover damages ranging from $500 to $100,000 per copyright infringed. If willful infringement for commercial advantages and private financial gain is proven, then criminal fines of up to $250,000 and/or a five-year prison sentence may apply—not worth the risk to the musician or the church!

What many do not seem to realize is that photocopying and then replacing those copies is much more expensive than purchasing the original scores. Plus, people tend to value an original piece of music with more pride and care. The excuses, which are many, are all inappropriate, unjustifiable, and do not exempt the musician or the church from the copyright laws:

- Our budget does not include money for sheet music.
- We have a very limited budget.
- The people will only lose the music.

- Music is too expensive.
- We sing too much music to purchase every composition that we sing.

There are acceptable ways of dealing with these types of issues rather than perpetuating the problem of continually photocopying and distributing music for performance. There are times, however, when permission may be granted to photocopy a piece of music:

- When a composition is permanently out of print and copies are no longer available, a publisher may grant permission for a limited number of copies to be made.
- When a composition is on backorder, a publisher may grant the director permission to photocopy the composition with the understanding that the photocopies will be destroyed and no longer used when the originals arrive.

Choir directors and members are taught to meticulously observe the correct notes, dynamics, accidentals, texts, and tempos, but disregarding the copyright on the printed music from which the choir sings is permissible and excusable.

lack of preparation for rehearsals

Another nonmusical issue choir directors face, although they are made aware of it and are evaluated consistently in their formal training, is not being sufficiently prepared for rehearsals. For example, choir directors themselves are often tardy for rehearsal, although they reprimand their members for tardiness. It is not uncommon for choir members to wait as long as fifteen or twenty minutes for the choir director to begin rehearsal, without notice, apology, or explanation from the director. Unfortunately, many directors wait until the last minute to make preparations for rehearsal because they consider it a low priority. This is apparent when sheet music is not in place or arranged for members upon their arrival, no repertoire schedule is posted or available, or choir members are asked what they would like to sing. Nothing could be more frustrating, insulting, and inconsiderate to the volunteer church choir members who willingly give their time and talents on a regular basis.

If one assumes the duties and responsibilities of choir director, then there is no excuse for such conduct and lack of commitment. Such behavior illustrates a lackadaisical and carefree attitude toward the organization and its mission, which makes it difficult to demand excellence of the choir. As director, you must lead by example!

There are a plethora of resources available to assist and guide choir directors in effective rehearsal planning and preparation, including musical resources, methods, vocal and instrumental literature in all styles and genres, videos, CDs, DVDs, and online instruction, which makes it impossible for a choir director to be unprepared. No conscientious, seriously committed, open-minded director can afford to ignore the many valuable resources that are available. To be certain, there are varying levels of quality and reliability, so we must sort through them to determine what is most useful and helpful to each of us.

various levels of musicianship, personality, and commitment

This brings me to a very sensitive issue: *musical* and *nonmusical* as it relates to musicians. Today, many churches and institutions are the unfortunate hostages of various levels of musicianship, personality, and commitment—and, as a choir director, that is challenging. In 1985, the late Wendell P. Whalum identified five categories of problematic music personnel serving in many churches.

Category 1. Talented but untrained musicians: These musicians often cannot read music, have no knowledge of choir organization or choral directing, and have no awareness of the historical importance of the hymns, liturgy, or religious service.

Category 2. Untrained and untalented but willing musicians: This group, larger in number than one would suspect, is made up of people who have had one or two years of piano study and are willing to accept leadership because no one in the church will or can assume responsibility for the music.

Category 3. Musicians with basic music training who accept church music duties without understanding what the program should be about and how it should be conducted: The result is that much of what is offered is out of focus with the needs and understanding of the congregation.

Category 4. Musicians with good training and previous exposure to excellent music who ignore the level of the congregation: Instead of educating the congregation, these musicians operate on a plane too sophisticated for the congregation. These musicians will frequently impose oratorios, cantatas, and pageants on people not yet educated in hymns and anthems who are, therefore, not ready for extended works.

Category 5. Musicians with excellent training who assume an attitude of superiority and make no attempt to lift [or broaden] the level of musical awareness: This kind of musician is usually identified as the organist-director who will officiate only at Sunday morning services or at the funerals and weddings of prominent citizens of the community.[3]

265

As painful and realistic as Whalum's categories are, they deserve our attention and consideration. In my career as a church and university choir director, my actions have put me into several of these categories, for which I have had to confess, repent, and "turn from my wicked ways."

I have been guilty of choosing music for the choir and congregation based on what I thought was appropriate to my training, my musical experience, my personal taste, and my understanding of "proper" liturgy and sacred music literature. My choices, however, did not take into consideration the people I was leading and serving or their culture, and often grossly failed to meet the needs of the worshipers or the worship service. Of course, I justified my decisions by insisting that I was committed to "lifting," "raising," and "elevating" the musical standards, which was a very narrow, prejudiced, and *vertical* choice of vocabulary and attitude. I have since learned that a *horizontal* vocabulary, which includes "augmenting," "expanding," "extending," and "increasing" the musical experiences and exposure, is much more appropriate, admirable, and pleasing to God.

We cannot adequately serve people we do not know or consider essential when planning music for the choir or congregation. The selection of music must not represent a personality, another church or choir, or a standard set by some outside group or organization; rather, the people must understand the text and the music to the extent that

266

it becomes incarnate in their lives and guides them through life's joys and challenges.

If we are to sing and pray (often at the same time) with spirit and understanding, then we must mean what we say and know what we mean. S. Paul Schilling once said, "Unless the hymns we use in worship express our convictions, we might as well sing the stock market reports, the real estate ads from the daily newspaper, or a list of names from the telephone directory.[4] The same holds true for anthems and arranged hymns and spirituals. Hymns and choral repertoire should become more than a group of songs and compositions that a choir and congregation have mastered and regularly performed. They should, as James Robert Davidson asserts, "instill the theological concepts as well as a devotional vocabulary which provide the catalyst for a feeling of community [and under-standing] in the proclamation of Christian truth through music."

I have also been guilty of imposing cantatas and other extended works on my choirs and congregations who needed a more diverse and inclusive hymnody, as well as an appreciation and understanding of anthems. One of the most important duties and responsibilities of the music director is to *educate* the congregation musically by teaching, illustrating, and providing a clear understanding of what is being sung and played in the church. It is insensitive to make no attempt to determine the level of the choir and congregation while

steadily inflicting a personal musical agenda or the taste of music preferred by a few on all.

Finally, I have also been guilty of asking who the deceased is or who is getting married before checking my availability to serve as organist for a funeral or wedding. I now see these as moral and ethical violations of my walk and my responsibility as a "minister of music" and a church musician.

loyalty and allegiance to the musician

Equally as sensitive in our walk is the unspoken need and expectation of loyalty, allegiance, and obligation from choir members above and beyond the expectations of the organization and its mission. It is unfortunate when a choir director's egocentric, narcissistic, and self-indulgent personality, insecurities, and psychological needs place on an unspoken but implicit loyalty, faithfulness, and allegiance on the choir members. I know choir directors who act as if they "own" their members, boasting of their loyalty to them even against the church leadership and other choirs and musicians. The need to control and manipulate people is dangerous and demands a serious revisiting of the calling of choir director or music director.

268

In some churches, the choir director's influence and decisions extend far beyond the realm of pastoral leadership. This is also often true in institutions where musical leadership has not changed for many years. The tendency is to feel a certain loyalty to the *person* without considering what is best or right for the church or institution. This type of behavior manifests itself by constantly being critical of and dismantling the work of other musicians, choirs, and musical organizations. The director constantly criticizes, finds fault, and attempts to destroy the work of others to elevate himself/herself. Eventually, the choir takes on the personality and superiority of the director and joins in the destruction. This is very prevalent, habitual, and typical of churches that have more than one choir or are considered one of the few outstanding choirs in the community and feel the need to diminish the others.

Using this unspoken influence, choir directors are able to convince members of their choir not the sing with other groups or participate in musical activities sponsored by other directors or groups. Members feel it is "unfaithful and unloyal" to cross the picket line established by their director. There are instances, perpetuated by musicians, where members are forbidden to attend worship services other than those at which they sing.

Such immoral, unethical, unprofessional, and childish behavior should be forbidden, discouraged, and not tolerated by church musicians. It is destructive, disconcerting, contemptuous, cynical, and violates every principle of Christianity. These are very unfortunate nonmusical considerations for church musicians that are alive and well in churches all over North America.

the relationship between pastor and musician

"It will remain bad theology so long as the theologian and the artist refuse to communicate with one another, as long as the theologian regards the artist as fundamentally a temperamental trifler, and the theologian as an obstinate and ignorant theorist, the best we shall get is patronage from church to music, together with tentative moralisms from musicians to musicians," Eric Routley wrote in his classic *Church Music and Theology.* "At worst it will be, as it often in practice is, a wicked waste of an opportunity of glorifying God through fruitful partnership."[5] If we substitute the word *pastor, minister,* or *priest* for "theologian" and the term *musician, minister of music, director of music,* or *choir director* for "artist," Routley's statement becomes more relevant and applicable.

It is unfortunate when a pastor and musician cannot and will not work together in a church. Few give little if any time to developing a strong and fruitful partnership. In some churches, the tension between pastor and musician is distracting and becomes the focus of the worship. This lack of communication, cooperation, and partnership leads to many distracted, disengaged, and meaningless worship experiences. Routley best called it a "wicked waste"! Successful partnerships begin with understanding, and productive partnerships rely on quality communication. Many people confuse talking with communicating. People think that the more they talk, the better they are communicating. But good communication begins when we stop talking and listen. Much of the time, we can improve our communication skills by listening more. "Talking at people," writes N. Lee Orr, "means we not only miss what they are saying but also risk misunderstanding their point of view. We then leave the encounter further convinced of how right we are, which hardens our position."[6] It is no wonder the other person is not enthusiastic or optimistic about future dialogue.

Orr continues, "Working partnerships between ministers and musicians result when both parties actively support the other, avoid public criticism of the other, ignore minor irritants, and work toward building a friendship."[7]

Pastors and musicians need to possess a rudimentary knowledge of the suppositions, skills, and vocabulary of each other's discipline. Without this knowledge, communication and partnership become difficult or even impossible, and even the best-intentioned efforts at collaborative ministry become strained.[8] "Clergy who have had excellent instruction in pastoral care often lack any sense of how to converse in a professional way with one of the single most important colleagues in their ministry: the church musician." Carol Doran and Thomas Troeger continue, "The story works in reverse as well: the musician, inexperienced in discussing theology and often feeling powerless, is fearful of beginning a conversation with the pastor about the way music functions in the liturgy. Sometimes musicians view their contributions entirely from the perspective of performance without considering how it fits with the liturgical and pastoral needs of the congregation."[9]

It is impossible for church musicians to develop, fortify, perpetuate, and strengthen their *walk* if they are not willing to walk with those to whom they are accountable and responsible. While it seems that protocol would make the pastor responsible for forging and establishing a partnership, it may be that the musicians should take the path less traveled and initiate the communication and partnership. The work of the Kingdom is so much greater than our egos, idiosyncrasies, agendas, and pride.

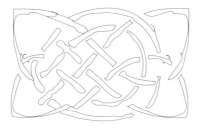

conclusion

Finally, the soul, the spirit, and the walk of the musician should be so visible, genuine, unpretentious, sincere, and truly incarnate in the total life of the musician that it serves as a model for all. I hasten to add that this is not to assume we as musicians are perfect, free from sin, and never tempted by the tsunamis, hurricanes, earthquakes, and wildfires of life. However, we cannot lead where we have not been. We cannot teach what we do not know. We cannot show the way to where we have never been. And we cannot talk of experiences we have never had. While many of these nonmusical considerations are blunt, candid, direct, head-on, point-blank, straightforward, and create a sense of discomfort, it is certainly not my intention to "tear down" but rather my hope and objective to "build up" for the Kingdom and Glory of God!

notes

1. James Abbington, *Let Mt. Zion Rejoice! Music in the African American Church* (Valley Forge, PA: Judson Press, 2001), 15.
2. James Robert Davidson, *A Dictionary of Protestant Church Music* (Metuchen, NJ: Scarecrow, 1975), 205–06.
3. The list is paraphrased from Wendell P. Whalum, "Music in the Churches of Black Americans: A Critical Statement," *The Black Perspective in Music* 14, no. 1 (Winter 1986), 16–7. This article also appears in *Readings in African American Church Music and Worship,* edited by James Abbington (Chicago: GIA, 2001), 503–04.

4. S. Paul Schilling, *The Faith We Sing* (Philadelphia, PA: Westminster, 1983), 23.

5. Eric Routley, *Church Music and Theology* (Philadelphia, PA: Muhlenberg, 1959), 110.

6. N. Lee Orr, *The Church Music Handbook for Pastors and Musicians* (Nashville, TN: Abingdon, 1991), 54.

7. Ibid., 67–70.

8. Carol Doran and Thomas H. Troeger, *Trouble at the Table* (Nashville, TN: Abingdon, 1992), 79.

9. Ibid., 78–83.

"...but an awareness of soul is also our ultimate goal."

"Landscape IV"

Chapter 24

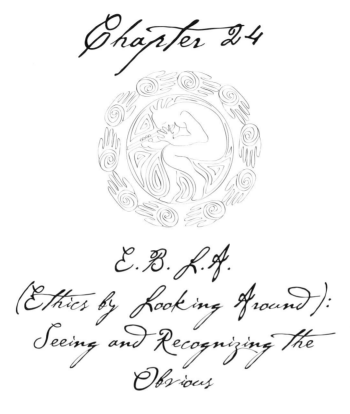

E. B. L. A.
(Ethics by Looking Around):
Seeing and Recognizing the
Obvious

The reasonable man adapts himself to the world: the unreasonable one persists in trying to adapt the world to himself.

Therefore all progress depends on the unreasonable man.

George Bernard Shaw

You must be the change you want to see in the world.

Mahatma Gandhi

276

It is a mistake to think of psychotherapy as the arena in which people change. When people say they want to change, I hear a subtle rejection of the person they are. I suppose that at some level, change is necessary—when life is tormenting, when one feels neurotic or psychotic, when a marriage is suffocating, when a job doesn't pay anything to the emotions. But even then, a conscious plan for change usually comes from the same imagination that got us in trouble in the first place. A new project of self-transformation may land back in the uncomfortable wallowing hole we just left.

When people talk about finding meaning in life, they imply that they can figure things out and set them right. But meaning that makes life worth living may be nothing more than a moment's realization, a  sensation, such as the touch of your baby's skin, or a sudden breathtaking appreciation of your home, or the passing thrill when you are reminded of your love for your spouse. Meaning may be an epiphany rather than an understanding. (pp. 122–123)

Thomas Moore
Original Self

The beyond is not what is infinitely remote, but what is nearest at hand. (p. 376)

Dietrich Bonhoeffer
Letters and Papers from Prison

The fundamental problem of ethics has been expressed as the question: What ought I do? The weakness of this formulation is in separating doing from the sheer being of the "I." As if the ethical problem were a special and added aspect of a person's existence. However, the moral issue is deeper and more intimately related to the self than doing. The very question: What ought I do? is a moral act. It is not a problem added to the self; it is the self as a problem. The moral problem can only be treated as a personal problem. How should I live the life that I am? My life is the task, the problem, the challenge.

The moral deed is important not only because the community, for example, needs it. It is important because without it there is no grasp of what is human about my being human. (p. 36)

Abraham Joshua Heschel
Who   Is   Man?

The divided life, at bottom, is not a failure of ethics. It is a failure of human wholeness. Doctors who are dismissive of patients, politicians who lie to the voters, executives who cheat retirees out of their savings, clerics who rob children of their well-being—these people, for the most part, do not lack ethical knowledge or convictions. They doubtless took courses on professional ethics and probably received top grades. They gave speeches and sermons on ethical issues and more than likely believed their own words. But they had a well-rehearsed habit of holding their own knowledge and beliefs at great remove from the living of their lives. (p. 7)

Parker J. Palmer
A   Hidden   Wholeness

*M*any perspectives have been offered on the subject of ethics for those of us who struggle with the challenges of the life of a musician/artist. But after writing and reading the advice of all my colleagues, one realization is clearly apparent to me. That realization is based, in part, on principles presented in *The Musician's Spirit* and *The Musician's Soul.* I suppose *The Musician's Soul* could be considered a required guide for the construction of an ethical code through self-realization and realizing the needs of people who make music with you. *The Musician's Spirit,* however, provides the tools for writing an ethical code that is meaningful and long-lasting.

I was struck by the realization that while we could all read and write a great deal on such a code of behavior for our "walk," the fact remains that if we look back at our lives, there have been persons in our lives who live the ethical codes we are all speaking to in this book. Moreover, these people come in and out of our lives. The sad fact is that for some reason within the human condition, we ignore such people and tend not to pattern our own lives after them. Reflection, appreciation, contemplation, and sheer awareness of another good soul close to us does not seem to be in our bag of equipment for life. These people may or may not be musicians. It really doesn't matter. Humane, kind, and loving behavior can be shown in all we do daily in the conduct of our lives.

The title of this chapter is "EBLA (Ethics by Looking Around)." What I am implying is that we stop and become aware of those people in our lives now who are living the ethical codes. Then examine the life you have already lived, and I think you will find there was not just one person but many. I don't think we consciously ignore the good work of such people, but the human psyche and ego are so powerful at times that our level of awareness is severely hindered or depleted for some reason. The principles that govern a good and caring person, regardless of what they do in life, work in all professions, especially music. Allow me to make my point with people in my life.

louis jordan

My father. Dad was an auto mechanic his entire life. He worked every day of his sixty-five years in his garage repairing people's vehicles. He worked alone, with no help. He was the son of Italian immigrants, who was orphaned at age three and adopted from an orphanage by another Italian immigrant family who already had six natural children and whose only means of income was the income of his adopted father (who was an umbrella repairman). My father's adopted mother died of cancer while my father was in high school. Dad married my mother, a nurse. (Author's note: I could just as well be writing about my own mother who spent her entire life helping everyone both as a part of her job and in her life.)

Anyone who has ever spent time in a small town garage will realize that it becomes a hub of activity for the locals. Dad's garage was always filled with a cast of characters that could have been sent from central casting in Hollywood: Jinx, Bogie, Jack the Mailman, Harry the Chief of Police, Sam, Little Richie, Hank. They all "hung out" at the garage and talked to my Dad as he worked on cars. As a person who was in the business of serving the public, he saw that the public could be difficult. It always seemed that a person's automobile brought out the worst in some people. Yet as I grew up, I saw my father show many remarkable kindnesses for others on a daily basis.

It seems as if every widow in town brought their car to Dad. Many times he repaired their cars and refused money or, for that fact, anything—baked goods or whatever—for his work. I asked Dad one time why he didn't charge a woman whose car was a particular challenge. He remarked, "Don't you think she has been through enough? This is the least I can do to help her." There were many times when someone's car was beyond repair. Knowing that the person had little or no resources, Dad would find a car, rebuild it, and give it to them. Dad never made a lot of money in that garage, but he seemed to get huge satisfaction from caring for people through their cars.

Now, here is the issue. My father was and remains one of the most ethically rooted people I have ever known. He treated everyone with care and compassion, and never spoke ill of anyone, even abusive customers. Only years after his passing do I realize what a great human being he was. Why was I not as aware as I am now of this man's way of living life and relating to people on a daily basis? Mostly it was a lack of awareness—an awareness of people around me.

Growing up, we believe somehow that we are the center of the universe and are blind to the good works of others, especially those close to us who we take for granted. That is the down side of the issue. The positive side is that despite our own personal ignorances and unawarenesses, spiritual osmosis does occur in our souls and spirits when such persons operate in our lives. Their deeds and goodness will impact our lives when we have the maturity of awareness to recall their effect on our lives and the impact they could have upon our way of being with each other. We must search for such influences because they also have a habit of receding into our consciousness, I suppose, because of the power of ego. Ego and, at times, raw human emotion cast a scrim over our perception so it is not possible to see the world clearly, or the effect of ourselves upon others. Awareness is a powerful tool that removes the perceptual scrim and allows us to live meaningful lives. Not only is a general type of awareness desirable in life, but an awareness of soul is also our ultimate goal. By being aware

282 of not only influential persons but also their very spirits and souls can we manifest changes in our daily ways of making music with others.

james steffy

James Steffy was the chair of the music department at Susquehanna University, where I did my undergraduate work. A more profound and influential presence one could not have wanted in one's life. However, at age twenty, I did not tend to notice these things. I never saw James Steffy act unkindly toward any student or colleague. It seemed as if he had boundless energy. He always had time for you, and when you spoke with him, you always felt as if you were the most important person to him. You also knew he would always be honest, even when the news was bad. And when the news was bad, he had a humane way of delivering the news that left both your soul and ego intact. He knew how to deal with people, students, colleagues, and musical ensembles. A graduate of Curtis on trombone, I believe my experiences playing in his band and wind ensemble are at the core of the way I make music, rehearse, and conduct a rehearsal to this day.

I began at Susquehanna University as a pre-med major. Unhappy, I wanted to change majors and become a music major. I prepared an audition and went through the audition process. The Monday after the audition, Steffy found me (no, he did not send me a note) and told me that I had not been accepted. He discussed several options with me, one of which was "to continue if your heart was driving your desires," explaining that the department would hear me again in a few months. The news was crushing. But I must say his spirit, words, and kindness gave me the energy to continue on.

Steffy would check with me during the intervening months, sticking his head in my practice room when walking through the practice hall wing. I felt that he always treated me as a person he respected, maybe even admired—not as the kid who had just failed an audition. He even gave me a key to the music building so I could enter the building at 4:00 each morning to practice.

I auditioned again. The dreaded Monday came. I saw Steffy approach me in the hall. He put his hand on my shoulder and said, "Well, Jim, it was better, but not quite there yet." I could feel the pall start to descend over my spirit, preparing for the inevitable words. He continued, "However, we are going to accept you. I just sense something in your spirit that will get you musically where you want to go. Your spirit is to be commended, and obviously, something is driving you to music. Work hard, and we will see where this will take you."

Throughout my undergraduate education, Steffy was there every step of my journey. In fact, when he was going through personal troubles with a divorce and a new life with someone I knew, he asked

284

for my support and understanding. I helped him and Nancy move into a fire hall that was their new makeshift home, a kind of loft space that Nancy made into a cozy place.

James Steffy was a shining example of EBLA. His every act, both musically and administratively, had a humane ring to it. It seems like he always knew "how to behave" within the herd, whether the herd was students, faculty, or his ensemble. I always felt respected in his presence. He was remarkable for his people skills and his understanding of the total education of a musician. His passionate dedication to all he did was infectious for all of us. But more importantly, he knew how to be with others, and he inspired all by his quiet competence.

And now, I wonder what Jim Steffy thinks. Retiring as the president of Muhlenberg College, I am sure he has no idea how profoundly his way of being has influenced my teaching life.

"...something in your spirit that will get you musically where you want to go."

"Tuzigoot Three"

Section Four
Journeying Out

"...we should be taught how to approach and handle the fears that confront us."

"Solitude"

Chapter 25

Be Not Afraid: Understanding Authentic Presence

As we become more obsessed with succeeding, or at least surviving, in that world, we lose touch with our souls and disappear into our roles. The child with a harmless after-school secret becomes the masked and armored adult—at considerable cost to self, to others, and to the world at large. It is a cost that can be itemized in ways well known to many of us:

- We sense that something is missing in our lives and search the world for it, not understanding that what is missing is us.
- We feel fraudulent, even invisible, because we are not in the world as who we really are.
- We project our inner darkness on others, making "enemies" of them and making the world a more dangerous place.
- Our contributions to the world—especially through the work we do—are tainted by duplicity and deprived of the life-giving energies of true self. (pp. 15–16)

There *are* selfish acts, to be sure. But those acts arise from an empty self, as we try to fill our emptiness in ways that harm others—or in ways that harm us and bring grief to those who care about us. When we are rooted in true self, we can act in ways that are life-giving for us and all whose lives we touch. (p. 39)

Parker J. Palmer

A Hidden Wholeness

Fear is fundamental to the human condition and to academic culture. We will always have our fears—but we need not be our fears.

I am fearful. I have fear. But I don't need to be here in my fear. I don't have to speak to you from my fear. I can choose a different place in me, a place of fellow feeling, of fellow traveling, of journeying together in some mystery that I know we share. I can "be not afraid" even while I have fear. (p. 57)

Parker Palmer

Living the Questions by Sam M. Intrator

This is the first, wildest, and wisest thing I know, that the soul exists, and that it is built entirely out of attentiveness. (p. 34)

Mary Oliver

"Low Tide"

The Amicus Journal

*P*erhaps the reason we have trouble with those around us is more basic than one would like to think. Conversely, approaches to handling these issues may be simpler than one might think. Musicians are certainly not exempt from the major obstacle to living and life that is a part of each one of us: fear. In *The Musician's Soul,* I presented the issue of fear as one of the reasons why we lack interiority, or have difficulty gaining entrance into ourselves because of the fears we carry with us daily. However, it is true that fear which is not dealt with internally will most certainly manifest itself externally through words, deeds, or sounds.

As part of our artistic education, we should be taught how to approach and handle the fears that confront us in our world so dominated by musicians and music. So many of us are afraid that relatively minor musical issues will cause us to be perceived by others as "weak" or poor musicians. These issues, while relatively minor, seem larger to us than they actually are. We also do not believe in our talents. We are always casting about and admiring what others can do and, in the process, lose sight of our own unique potential. We are also surrounded by what Julia Cameron refers to as "crazymakers"—persons who spend much of their daily energies making others feel bad so that they appear more talented in the eyes of others (as well as their own). Unable to deflect such energies, many of us live with the constant fear that we are simply not good enough to do what we are doing.

I asked Weston Noble in one of our many conversations what was the guiding rule for his teaching, whether in the classroom or rehearsal room. He stated simply that it was *affirmation*. He remarked that everyone needs to be affirmed; it is that constant and continual affirmation that allows persons to realize their potential as musicians and teachers. Affirmation. What a strange concept! Imagine if many of us spent much of our time affirming ourselves and being affirmed how different a musical world we might occupy! Since Weston shared that tidbit of information with me, I have pondered the powerful impact it can have not only upon others, but also on ourselves.

affirming awareness

It seems to me that affirmation, while by itself is admirable, probably is not sufficient for long-term growth and musical deepening without additional help of some kind. While affirming others or ourselves, I think it is crucial that we maintain a state of *constant awareness* about both ourselves and our place in the world. We fall into ethical dilemmas because we turn inward and lose awareness of the larger world. Unawareness breeds profound fears. In turn, that unawareness causes a dulling of the creative fire and honest spontaneity.

I have witnessed it over and over again in the musicians I know   **293**

and have taught. They make huge musical relationship blunders with

themselves and the people with whom they make music when they

lose the perception of the world around them and all the people they

come in contact with. Music becomes an intense "focus-

ing" act, where they focus on every minute detail but

seem to lose touch with the larger picture. Allow me to

use a simple illustration.

I know conductors who pride themselves on "memorizing" their

scores. I am not sure they are truly memorizing their scores. The fact

of the matter is we do not memorize scores. Rather, we recall sounds

we have made familiar through study and rehearsal. I believe that

persons who use this technique use it as a mask for a type of

psychological control over the ensemble, which creates a false sense

of security. That false sense of security actually erects a wall between

those conductors and their ensembles. My proof of this is in the

sound of the performance. The sound is never warm or spontaneous.

There is always a certain type of aggressiveness in the sound of the

ensemble, and there seems to be a rigid inflexible element in the

rhythm of the piece primarily because the "focus" is totally on the

mechanical elements of the score. Such conductors lose awareness of

everything that is going on at the moment outside of the notes and

rhythms of the score. Memorization alone is insufficient; recalling a score in the atmosphere of total awareness will breed far different results. Conductors lose awareness of their bodies and of their "human-ness." Fear empowers the "memorization" to overcome the musical "ills" of the ensemble. Consequently, the conductors never really hear the root difficulties in the ensemble.

Being reminded of the "fear factor" in our lives, many of us will not argue about either its presence or its power over us. With that acknowledgment comes a certain kind of empowerment for change, if one commits to it. As I spoke at great lengths in *The Musician's Soul,* one of the most effective antidotes to counter fear in one's life is love of one's self. Love of self begins an empowerment that unearths one's true musical and human gifts, which allows for the power of those gifts to be manifest. Perhaps what Weston Noble was referring to could be called "loving affirmation of the self."

Instead, I have met too many people who suffer from an empty self. They have a bottomless pit where their identity should be—an inner void they try to fill with competitive success, consumerism, sexism, racism, or anything that might give them the illusion of being better than others. We embrace attitudes and practices such as these not because we regard ourselves as superior but because we have no sense of self at all. Putting others down becomes a path to identity, a path we would not need to walk if we knew who we were. (p. 38)

Parker J. Palmer

A Hidden Wholeness

In Chapter 21, "One Body, Two Selves," I shared a current neurological viewpoint that counters the recent "whole brain" theories that dot the landscape of educational psychology and many methods classes in music education. Perhaps "One Body, Two Selves" may make one a bit fearful. And perhaps fear, in various forms, may be the basis for some poor ethical choices.

Fear depletes human energies—energies that are core to any musician's walk. As a conductor and performer, the amount of energy that is "sent" into the ensemble during either a rehearsal or a concert is, at times, simply astounding. Without that constant sharing of abundant energy, rehearsals and performances are dull and lackluster. The type of energy I am speaking of is not the outward energy displayed in excessive physical movement but rather the constant burning of a warm inner core that is omnipresent to all of those who come in contact with you. Leonard Bernstein believed that the primary "job" of the conductor was to provide a warm human core at the front of the ensemble. Those who believe in the power of Vortex energy centers of the earth assert that virtual waves of energy are emitted from the earth in the form of funnels of energy. These are strong magnetic fields that both recharge individuals and realign the energy channels in the body. In Sedona, Arizona, there are several such energy vortexes. By visiting them, one can experience a noticeable "recharge" in one's energy core.

However, because of the energy depletion that worry and fear cause in musicians, we must acquire means by which to recharge and, consequently, reaffirm ourselves almost on a daily basis. One method I would like to suggest to musicians (especially conductors) is the ancient Chinese practice of *QiGong* (pronounced *chee-gong*). I found that even after one session of this ancient meditative and energy practice, I felt energized and renewed. I was amazed to find that the practices had much in common with my training as a conductor. In fact, the skill for acquiring "Qi" (or energy) through this practice has proven to be a valuable daily tool for me. Aside from the valuable energy aspects of the art, there are many additional health benefits.

a QiGong primer for musicians: cultivating Qi

Without appearing as a fanatic of New Age practices, I believe musicians become afflicted and compromised for some very simple reasons. A human being is simply incapable of giving out energy on a daily basis in practice, rehearsal, or performance without replenishing those "stores" of energy at some point during the day or week. To risk working in an artistic environment with such depleted energy stores produces an instability that results in reactions that may be unpredictable depending upon the circumstances. Any practice that could maintain our contact with the larger world while restoring needed energy is certainly worth our most serious consideration.

There also can be no doubt about various meditative/physical studies and/or practices that allow body, mind, and spirit to maintain contact with each other. Yoga practitioners will sing the praises of its constant practice and integration into one's life style. Tae kwon do practitioners will tout its benefit to overall mental and spiritual health, and its abilities to center oneself and one's energies. The practice of Alexander Technique has gained many musician practitioners because of the body awareness it teaches. Many musicians stumble into the benefits of these practices after they encounter some type of "stress" and "tension" that, in turn, impacts their music making.

Perhaps it is time for the music profession to study and embrace those practices that have the potential to "recharge" the body, spirit, and mind of the musician. And perhaps one of the roots of our many problems as musicians in our dealings with others is that the practice of our art leaves our spirits and bodies so depleted of energy that little remains within us when it is needed to see ourselves through challenging or pressing human and/or musical situations.

I would like to present here a relatively new viewpoint on the use of the ancient practice of the Chinese healing practice of QiGong as just such a vehicle for all musicians.[1] QiGong seems to be at least one practice that can lead to a replenishment of musician energy stores through acquisition of the energy of Qi.[2]

what is QiGong?

In my opinion, this phenomenon (of QiGong) can be compared with the launching and receiving principle in radio, for it is a special "field" in objective reality. If only you know how to receive *Qi* with the corresponding specific means, you can receive *Qi* to obtain its curing effect. (p. 68)

Ou Wen Wei

Pan Gu Mystical QiGong

If there is one concept that comes up in all forms of Chinese medicine it is that of Qi, or vital energy. Qi is the very backbone of the Chinese healing arts. It refers to the energy of the Universe that is channeled from nature and runs through all of us. To have Qi is to be alive, while to have none is to be dead.

QiGong also relies on the manipulation of this vital energy. This is done through "meridians," channels that pass through all the vital organs of the body. There are twelve of these meridians, which correspond to twelve organs. These meridians are interconnected, so that one runs into the other and passes through the body like an invisible river of energy. Anyone can learn simple exercises to manipulate his or her own Qi. This practice is known as *internal* QiGong. (p. xiii)

The root of the way of life, of birth and change, is Qi; the myriad things of heaven and earth all obey this law. Thus Qi in the periphery envelops heaven and earth. Qi in the interior activates them. The source wherefrom the sun, moon, and stars derive their light, the thunder, rain, wind and cloud their being, the four seasons and the myriad things their birth, growth, gathering and storing; all this is brought about by Qi. Man's possession of life is completely dependent upon this Qi. (pp. 283–284)

Master Hong Liu
The Healing Art of QiGong

Let me try to summarize both the practice of QiGong and its benefits to musicians at the risk of over-simplifying the concepts of this practice.[3] Basically stated, the mind/body exercises as advocated by this specific practice of QiGong allow the body to function in parallel as a type of radio device. Through QiGong, one learns to use the body as a "receiver" of energy or Qi that is constantly around us. This energy is carried in atoms and particles energized by the sun and moon that are available for our "collection." The exercises are the collection devices that allow us as musicians to "recharge" and "refocus," with direct benefits upon our physical, mental, and spiritual health. Acquisition of Qi may be felt as vitality. At times, one can feel a certain magnetic or energy force between one's hands. Most importantly, acquiring Qi possesses both conscious action and super-conscious action.

Again, at the risk of sounding very New Age, QiGong aims at achieving within oneself a certain balance and harmony of the energy that is *around* you and *within* you. The energy within you can only be replenished from sources that are external to you. QiGong provides a way of harvesting the energy that is omnipresent in the environment around you. The key to acquisition is a mind that is calm and a spirit that is open and loving. Finally, QiGong teaches body positions that maximize this energy acquisition.

A parallel to this principle can be found in biology. The growth of plants (and to a certain extent, living things in another chemical context) requires the use of the energy of the sun and photosynthesis. Photosynthesis converts solar energy into life-giving energy and food for plant life. The practice of QiGong allows for the acquisition of beneficial energies of the sun and moon to repair and revitalize the soul, spirit, and body in a powerful and direct way.

energy flow in QiGong

One of the most valuable images necessary in the practice of QiGong is the concept of energy. This image is especially valuable for conductors and musicians. When visualizing the flow of energy throughout the body, we must visualize that the energy flows through the entire body like water. This flow is constant, and its speed is directly relational to the amount of external energy that can be brought into the body. Stated another way, we must be in a constant state of awareness of our entire body in order for energy to flow throughout all parts of our body in this way. Unawareness leads to severe blockages in energy which, in turn, will manifest themselves in human interaction problems and musical issues.

QiGong is another vehicle by which we as musicians can maintain a state of constant physical awareness. Physical awareness is the catalyst for spiritual awareness (to be discussed in the pages that follow). The goal is for musicians to acquire the skills by which energy acquisition becomes habitual and that feeling of liquid energy flow within the body is both a constant and a norm for our daily existence.

The one concept that I have found most difficult to impart to both my choirs and conductors is how "energy" flows through the body. Many believe that the body is a vibrating mass of protoplasm—

302

that energy somehow reaches the ensemble by sheer power of perception. That perception will, with certainty, lead to a minimal transference of energy to ensemble, instrument, or audience.

Many others believe that energy is generated from a furnace-like source in the body and then is, almost literally, "hurled" or thrown out at the ensemble ("energy implosion"). Such a bombardment usually has the opposite effect. It usually creates a driven, aggressive sound in the choir. Such energy dispersion is also the product of persons who are unable to "let go" and trust themselves or their ensemble. They believe that music "is made" rather than being a reaction as a result of correct energy transference to the ensemble. These persons are perceived as being "energetic," but their energy generally has a detrimental effect upon the musicians they come in contact with. There is also another characteristic of such persons that has direct bearing on the musician's walk. I have observed that such energy flow, because of its inward and cumulative effect, often breeds frustration. Energy "held within" ourselves becomes so powerful that it turns us on ourselves, and frustration and a type of "nervousness" and impatience are the by-products because the "energy" is not being used.

An analogy might be helpful. One of the older homes I lived in came equipped with a coal insert for the fireplace. This insert was equipped with sliding iron shutters on the front door to allow for

proper ventilation of the coal fire. Once when I added coal to the fire,

I neglected to open the vents. I left the room and returned about

twenty minutes later, and the entire insert glowed red hot! Not until I

opened the vents and allowed heat into the room did the metal cool

to its normal color and state. Musicians who do not either practice or

conceptualize the correct flow of energy constantly "overheat." This

"overheating" needs to be eliminated from the body through some

type of "cool down." Unfortunately for many of us, we get rid of this

overheated and misdirected energy in many negative ways.[4]

two paradigms for energy sharing or dispersion for musicians

Two of the most helpful paradigms I have found to support this

energy dispersion process are as follows. In QiGong, one of the paths

of energy through the body is called the "fire path."[5] The path runs

down the center of the body from the forehead toward the outside of

the body cavity, down through the pelvis, upward along the spine,

around the back of the skull, and completes its cycle over the top of

the skull. This energy flow, if allowed to occur, is constant. Energy is

then shared in two ways with other musicians.

First, the most powerful transference of energy occurs from the circulation of energy that travels along the external core of the body. If the arms are used correctly by the conductor, the center of the body is left "open" for that energy to be both sent and perceived by the ensemble.[6] That energy is sensed like a vertical pillar or rod from the pelvis upward to the top of the head.[7] This is a powerful energy core that must be kept "open" and "free" as much as possible.

Second, other energy or Qi is transferred through the arms and out to the ensemble through the palms of the hands. This is possible because the arms are connected to the body energy circulation via the sternoclavicular joint.[8] The proper perception of both of these paths of energy circulation are essential for the maintenance of a healthy "energy" and sharing of that energy (Qi) in a healthy way with the ensemble. Examine the illustration below and note the direction of the arrows that detail the overall pattern of energy flow throughout the body.

Pattern of Energy Circulation in the Body: Side View

the danger of energy implosion for musicians

One of the root problems in the musician's walk is an inability to channel the energy that musicians have in a healthy way. While many of us have been taught as artists to "send" energy to the ensemble and to the audience, there seems to have been little instruction on how to route that energy through the body or how to acquire more stores of energy when the supply is depleted for one reason or another.

Imploded energy sets off a chain reaction within musicians that can be self-mutilating, frustrating, and hurtful to those who surround us. How does imploded energy feel within us? It results in restlessness, unhappiness, frustration, anger in varying degrees, inordinate self-criticism, frustration with others, and a general level of impatience with all those who "get in the way" of the music. Understand that we don't mean to do this. But in our own defense, to my knowledge no one has ever discussed the healthy and desirable path of energy through the body and out of the body. Energy used and acquired through these pathways is rejuvenating and invigorating. Energy channeled incorrectly leads to depression and dark moods that, invariably, have detrimental effects on the music we make and the people we love.

306

The solution is simple. Perception and correct mapping of the energy flow though the body and out of the body is key. When energy flow is correct, much good musical work and human work follows in kind. For me, QiGong has provided a valuable vehicle to solve this crucial puzzle in the musician's walk. If we examine any musicians who are admired, impeded energy flow is not a characteristic of their being. For some reason, either through the persons they are or the lives they have lived, energy always flows from them to others in a fluid, effortless way. I believe this is so because it channels through them in a correct way and its flow outward is not impeded in any way whatsoever.

energy circulation applied to ensembles

Recently, I have come to believe that the concept of energy flow should be taught to ensembles. While individual musicians can be helped with this paradigm, its effects can be logarithmically multiplied when applied to larger groups of musicians. The danger with any ensemble is that in the heat of performance or rehearsal, energy flow is impeded or blocked. Sound is not as vibrant as it could be, and pitch problems become the norm. One of the root problems of intonation difficulties is impeded energy flow within individual

musicians. Conductors would do well to discuss energy flow with their ensembles and show them the diagram on page 304. If possible, have them also perform music from the QiGong starting position!

the basic QiGong exercise sequence: the twenty-six repetitions

In the specific practice of QiGong, the following exercises are performed sequentially.[9] Slow and constant movement is the key to ample energy acquisition. Twenty-six repetitions are required for each movement. This number is based upon spiritual numerology. A verbal recitation at the beginning and end of the exercise sequence frames the entire repetition sequence.

A prerequisite to all of these exercises is a sense of core body alignment. An approach to core alignment can be found in *Learn Conducting Technique with the Swiss Exercise Ball* (GIA, 2004). In fact, one can best arrive at the core alignment of one's body through awarenesses gathered from sitting on a Swiss exercise ball, as described in that text. Being organized like an apple around a core, where the core is one's pelvis, is central to vital energy flow through the body. Without organizing one's body around its core, it will be difficult—if not impossible—to experience the free flow of energy throughout the body. At all times during these exercises, awareness of one's alignment and body core must be maintained through constant body awareness. The following alignment is necessary for this to happen during the execution of the QiGong exercises.

Proper images for breathing should be employed at all times. The correct process for breathing is detailed in *Evoking Sound: Body Mapping and Basic Patterns for Conductors* (GIA, 2002). Body

Mapping, as demonstrated with the eight-handed breathing exercise, is central to this process. Throughout all of the exercises, it is most important to remember that the air comes into the body in a wavelike motion from top to bottom. Exhalation also occurs in a wavelike motion from top to bottom.

For those interested in gaining a deeper understanding and, consequently, benefit from QiGong, it is widely believed that a practice unique to QiGong should be studied and mastered. This breathing technique attempts to wed breath with spirit. Obviously, such a technique would be beneficial to musicians.[10]

Before we enter this practice, I must emphasize one more thing. That is the entire embryonic breathing practice occurs through inner self-observation. That means "self inner feeling." This feeling is the way your mind communicates with your physical body, Qi and Shen. This feeling can be shallow or profound, depending on how much you are able to calm your mind down and feel it. The level of feeling is unlimited, and normally follows the depth of your mind and awareness. Naturally, wrong feeling or mental perception can also lead you into fascination, illusion, and imagination. These false and unrealistic feelings can lead you to a state of emotional disturbance, and further away from the correct practice of Qi cultivation. (p. 323)

Jwing-Ming Yang
QiGong Meditation

All the exercises must be performed in a slow tempo, between approximately quarter = 42 and quarter = 60. The speed of the movement in the hands must be both constant and unvarying. It is the constant slow speed of the hand movements that allows one to both feel and gather energy from the atmosphere surrounding one's hands. Control and maintenance of a consistent speed is most important in the performance of the exercise sequence. And remember, twenty-six repetitions for each exercise!

starting position and recitation

Starting position is most important. The palms up position of the hands allows for energy or Qi to enter the body and, in essence, recharge it (see Figure 1). The belief is that energy enters the energy meridians of the body through the palms. Approximately two minutes should be spent in this position as one focuses one's thought on the breath, devoid of ego. To assist in getting ego out of the way and beginning the proper flow of energy, many practitioners of QiGong encourage an out-loud recitation. This recitation, no matter its form, should include elements of giving, sharing, acquiring, and love. A sample of such a recitation follows:

311

Take kindness and benevolence as basis;
Take frankness and friendliness as bosom.
Speak with reason; Treat with courtesy;
Move with emotion; Act with result.[11]

Figure 1
Starting Position and Recitation

left side motion

Move to the position shown in Figure 2, where the hands are parallel on the left side of the body. The hands should be no more than sixteen inches apart. Move the hands in a slow and circular clockwise motion, with the lower hand following the motion of the upper hand, but slightly behind the upper hand. This should be performed with one complete rotation every two seconds. Twenty-six complete cycles should be performed.

Figure 2
Left Side Motion

312

motion transfer from left to right

After the twenty-six rotations are completed, move both hands to the center of the body, parallel with the navel (see Figure 3). Transition the same position to the right side of the body . As you transition, the hand that was on the bottom is now on the top, on the right side of the body.

Figure 3
Motion Transfer from Left to Right

right side motion

Perform the same circular motion with the left hand on top, and the right following it (see Figure 4). This should be performed with one complete rotation every two seconds. Twenty-six complete cycles should be performed.

Figure 4
Right Side Motion

middle motion

After the motion has been completed on the right side of the body, turn the hands so they are parallel with the mid-line of the body (see Figure 5). Then rotate the hands, one following the other, for twenty-six forward rotations, with each rotation taking at least two seconds. The slower the rotations, the greater the benefit.

Figure 5
Middle Motion

drawing open motion

After the repetitions have been completed in middle motion, still the hands. Open the arms slowly while inhalating (see Figure 6).

Figure 6
Drawing Open Motion

314

drawing close motion

After exhaling and moving to the drawn open position, return to the middle position while exhaling, arriving at a flower or "cupped" position of the hands (see Figure 7).

Figure 7
Drawing Close Motion

flower/focusing motion

After the drawing close motion, bring the hands into a cupped position as if they are holding a flower. This hand position should mirror the position of the chin line and be approximately two to four inches below the chin (see Figure 8). Stay in this position for approximately two minutes. If time permits, repeat the entire sequence again.

Figure 8
Flower Motion
(Focusing Motion)

acquiring, understanding, and practicing authentic presence

In reading Parker Palmer's most recent book, *A Hidden Wholeness* (Jossey-Bass, 2004), I was struck by an analogy, or rather a life situation, in the book that may hold one of the keys for us as artists. While Palmer has a viewpoint on this subject, I would like to draw a slightly different parallel for musicians and artists. I found it remarkable that before I had ever read this book, I had pondered the exact same situation and tried to reason through what these "new" feelings were. Palmer brought clarity to my visions and feelings; I encourage you to read his account, but I would like to share my perspective with you.[12]

I believe that if one can combine the mimetical state suggested in *The Musician's Soul* with the "authentic presence" described below, both of these paradigms detail the "door inward" to many answers needed for the musician's walk. The combination of the two constitutes a balanced state of awareness for music making. Once achieved, I believe that not only relationships with other musicians but also one's music making will ascend to inspired and profound human expression.

understanding authentic presence

Along with the powerful idea of awareness as discussed earlier, it might be helpful to try to describe what it "feels" like to be in that heightened and aware state. At this writing, it will be almost two years since my mother passed after a long and painful battle with cancer. I must admit I found the whole "situation" very difficult to deal with. My sister, a nurse, was a godsend in this situation. She was strong where I was weak and ineffective. My mother's companion, Charlie, was also more infinitely effective in helping my mother. Many times I felt angry because I felt conflict between the deep love I had for my mother and my total inability to deal with the realities of life that were present. Helplessness seemed to be a dominating emotion. The immediate result for me, ironically, was physical illness. The illness provided me with a convenient way to be both physically and spiritually absent.

My schedule at school, grueling as usual, was compounded by inhumane situations that I would rather not discuss. In my phone conversations with my Mom, I could hear the pain in her voice and her desperation. I tried to calm her with my words. But because I did not understand this idea of authentic presence, I could be of no help to her.

I was jolted out of self-imposed isolation one day when she called me. In essence, she forced me into a type of action or state that authentic presence brings. She called to tell me how much pain she was in. The cancer in her lower spine was unbearable. She told me she could no longer lie down. She had sat at our family kitchen table for over a week, eating and sleeping there because she could no longer lie prone. I cried silently on the other end of the phone. And then she did it. She said. "Jim, I am sitting here at this table waiting to die; I cannot bear it anymore."

I called my sister immediately. By the next afternoon, hospice had been contacted and Mom had a bed in the living room. For the first time in many weeks, she could lay prone and sleep. Increased medication helped. In a few days, I was well enough to go and visit.

I will try to describe what is essentially indescribable. It is that very same feeling I now realize through the help of Parker Palmer that I have when, I believe, artistic music making occurs. I am paraphrasing Palmer's concept and calling it "authentic presence." The difference is a bit semantical, but I think it is an important distinction for musicians.

As I approached the front door of my mother's home, my stomach turned with fear. I had to force myself up what seemed the endless two steps to the porch. When I walked into the house, Mom lay there, very calm and semi-sedated. She heard my voice and we

318   reached for each other. I tried to speak but could not; it was like I had nothing to say. All I felt was an incredible sense of love and an abiding calm in her presence. How odd. I believed that I would bring her "support" and "calm," yet she was the calm presence in that room. My Aunt Joyce, Charlie, and I sat for what was about an hour and half and said almost nothing. While the situation would have been previously labeled as "sad" by me, I found myself in an incredibly heightened state of being—a state of *authentic awareness.* Looking back, it was a strange alchemy of love and calm acceptance, and it was truly, stunningly beautiful. It is a wordless calm combined with a humble place. Two years later, I realize that when I am at my best musical place, I have that same feeling. And now I try to go there...every rehearsal, every performance, every class. It is what I am calling *authentic presence.* It was what Martin Buber, I believe, meant in part in trying to describe "I and thou."

Mom passed about nine days later, with her family and best life friends at her side in a room that was stunningly quiet on a bright and beautiful Spring day in March. God ended her suffering and left us all a gift...the gift of authentic awareness. Ironic, isn't it? You learn what life is through one's passing to the next place.

One strange aside: I avoided even thinking or rehashing those days for many weeks. As we cleaned out my family's homestead, there was one item left on the first floor: the Victorian claw-footed kitchen

ᴷᴸᵃᵂ ₛ'ₙₐᵢᵢₛᵤM ₔdT

table. It was the table my father died at. It was the table my mother suffered at. Since I gave it to my parents, my sister said I should take it. I had told my wife that I was going to send it to auction. I didn't want it in the house. It was too painful. She was insistent, and I gave in. That table is now in the family room in my home, and I now must publicly confess that it is my favorite spot to study scores and to just touch. Because of the experiences it represents, it allows me an express "ticket" to a strong and abiding feeling of authentic presence. Let it be known: In rehearsal, concerts, and classes, I am always imagining myself with my Mom in those final days. The table is my vehicle for that now frequent, almost daily, journey. I realize that it is not enough to love others. The power in that love is to be serenely aware so musicians can hear and give of their gifts and their spirit. I learned how not to fear from being fearful—an ironic and profound twist that is one of life's great lessons.

Search your own life for your authentic awareness situation and you, too, will have arrived at a better place for your art.

Requiem aeternam, Florence.

Pax, James.

"Search your own life for your authentic awareness."

"Sunset VI"

notes

1. I was first introduced to this practice in Sedona, Arizona, at the MiiAmo Spa. After one class, I immediately felt the results of this relatively simple and direct approach taught by Paulette, who is on the staff of that spa. I was also impressed because many of its central principles were not only easily acquired in one class but were directly in line with the principles that I believe are centrally important to the art of conducting.

2. My first familiarity with the term "Qi" (pronounced *chee*) was in my acquaintance with a school of conducting pedagogy in Japan where there are a minimum number of gestures taught. All gestures are taught as movement toward or away from the Qi. This Qi point is what has been referred to in the Western World as the "ictus."

3. I would encourage readers who are interested in acquiring these skills for this practice to not only find a practitioner in QiGong (available at www.Pangushengong.org) but to also read and study the concise book by Ou Wen Wei, *Pan Gu Mystical QiGong.*

4. In *The Musician's Soul*, the concept of mimetics certainly is a synonym for what is being described here. Conscious thought is similar to the vent doors in the coal furnace. Conscious thought of love and care begins to channel life energies in a positive direction to other musicians or the ensemble.

5. Yang, *The Root of Chinese QiGong*, p. 85.

6. The correct use of the arms is dealt with extensively in the text, *Learn Conducting Technique with the Swiss Exercise Ball.* The reader is highly encouraged to read the section regarding the axis of both right and left arms.

7. Also remember that the eyes are immediately adjacent to this pillar of energy and play their own role in the sharing of vital energies.

8. The sternoclavicular joint is described and mapped on the DVD by Heather Buchanan and the author, *Body Mapping and Basic Conducting Patterns.* It is essential that the entire arm and its structure be understood and mapped if one desires appropriate energy flow to be shared with the ensemble.

9. For readers desiring additional detail, two sources should be consulted. *Pan Gu Mystical QiGong*, by Ou Wen Wei, offers a detailed, step-by-step description of this approach to QiGong, which is recommended by the author. I would also encourage readers to visit the Web site of the Pan Gu Shengong International Research Institute: www.pangushengong.org.

10. For those interested in such an insight, the reader is referred to Chapter 5, "The Practice of Embryonic Breathing," in the book by Yang entitled *QiGong Meditation: Embryonic Breathing.*

11. Ou Wen Wei from title page *of Pan Gu Mystical QiGong.*

12. Readers of this book are strongly encouraged to read Parker Palmer's book, *A Hidden Wholeness* (Jossey-Bass, 2004). This incredible book may provide additional strategies for a musician's walk. Of particular interest are the sections that describe the Möbius strip, referred to by Palmer as his "Quaker PowerPoint." The Möbius strip analogy contains a powerful paradigm for conductors and musicians of all types. I highly encourage every reader to read and study this remarkable book.

"The writing of an ethical code can also serve as a clear path for the future."

"Fork in the Road"

Chapter 26

Dedicating Oneself to an Ethical Code

Know that you are both intelligent and stupid, often in the same moment. Admit to what you desire and what you fear. If you did little more than these two things, you would be filled with irony and your actions would be infinitely more trustworthy for their honesty. It's all right to have grand and eccentric longings. It's all right to be afraid. Only by embracing these two emotional pillars will you glimpse the nature of your soul, which is the ground of your existence. (p. 114)

Thomas Moore
Dark Nights of the Soul

It seems to me (and to increasingly greater numbers of people) that *all* the major religions have failed in one essential task—the reducing of human anxiety and aggression through the instruction of human beings in their essential divine nature. Each of them, in different but fundamentally similar ways, controls believers and claims to broker the relationship between the believer and God in ways that both subtly and blatantly keep the believer from claiming the full range of his or her divine powers. (p. 25)

Andrew Harvey
The Direct Path

It is then that this educational/artistic spiral of institutional competition, private teacher pressure, and individual misperceptions does the most damage. Young musicians often become seriously despondent, incapable of remembering the very reason they went into music in the first place; that is, to practice an art to which they are completely dedicated and that they love with a passion. As the head of an institution whose mission is to educate the performing artist of the future, I believe it is of the utmost importance to create an artistic and educational environment that provides high-quality professional performance training, as well as elements that nurture not only a complete performer, but also a complete human being.

Joseph W. Polisi
The Artist As Citizen

$\mathcal{T}$he case has been made to support the need for an ethical code to help guide us through our professional lives and to ensure a better state of music making. The case has also been made for the possible contents of such a code—not only by myself, but also by others with a certain life and professional perspective. The case has further been made for the extraction of a code of ethics from those persons who are immediately in our life experiences, who may be easily observable and who we can benefit from.

I am hopeful that in the coming years, the professional organizations that surround our professional lives will take strides to develop a code of ethics for the musicians who work in schools, churches, and with other musicians. However, until that time, their work must truly be our own. As individuals, we must commit ourselves to our own personal code of ethics that will guide our living and interaction as we deal with others in our musical existence. Each one of us may assume this responsibility. I am suggesting that after reading this book, each of you write your own code of ethics and then abide by it with prescribed checks and balances.

For those of you who are new to the profession, you will need to rely on the material in this book and trust in the suggestions from others with considerably more life and professional experience to chart your way. The wisdom of many persons is contained in these pages. I wish I had had such a resource at my fingertips when I began my teaching career.

For those of you who have experience, the exercise of writing your ethical code will be painful at times, for it will involve confession of wrongdoings each of us has done while on our professional "path." This acknowledgment and realization is necessary and good.

The writing of an ethical code can also serve as a clear path for the future. Each of us needs to develop a strict list of "rules" that will guide our behavior with others when times become difficult. We must be ultimately responsible for our behavior with "the herd." We must also realize that if we do not accept this responsibility, not only will we hurt people with whom we come into contact, but the music we make will also suffer irreparable damage.

It is this last fact that many musicians are oblivious to. They treat their ensembles and people around them inhumanely. Yet they seem to believe that because they do it "for the music," the music they make will not suffer. How foolish. With those I have known who seem to throw ethical concerns to the wind, their music reflects their contempt for others. The sad realization about these persons is that they never hear the effects of their life actions on others or their music.

numbing down

On days when I have been unkind to others, I can hear my spirit in the music that comes back at me from my ensemble. That sound has been my most sobering teacher. That sound has been the negative rein-

forcement necessary to cause me to consider altering my ethical path.

There is a double-edged sword in all of this. I am convinced that

for the early years of my career, I did not listen to my ensembles. I

most certainly heard them, but I did not listen. I did not listen because

I was unaware to some degree of the relationships I had with

colleagues and my students—a kind of "numbing down." I was numb

and unaware part of the time. It was during those times of numbness

and unawareness that I ignored or minimalized the power of

relationships with others and their impact on my music making.

When I began listening to my choirs, it was then and only then that I

began to see the intimate connection between the sound of my

ensemble and the ethical behavior of my ways. It was both a sobering

and revelatory event in my life.

You must first realize that the sound of your ensemble *is* your

teacher. Writing of an ethical code will be of no use until it is put to

the test others make daily of being exposed to actively interactive

sound.

With that being understood, it is now time for you to commit to

writing your ethical code. I would like to suggest the following

procedure for constructing such a code:

James Jordan

328

1. Take those things from this book that have resonated with you and your life.

2. Identify a person in your life (not necessarily—and probably not—a musician) who has profoundly affected your way of being.

3. Make a separate list of times when other musicians hurt you. Devote a portion of your ethical code to "rules" that would enable you to avoid that behavior.

4. Make a separate list of times when you may have been hurtful to other musicians and artists. Devote a portion of your ethical code to "rules" that will point you away from those tendencies in the future.

5. Complete your ethical code by developing a "wish list" of rules of conduct that you gather from reading and life experience.

monitoring, maintaining, and policing your code: an ethical advisor

Many professions that have ethical codes have a mechanism for monitoring members of that organization and holding them to a higher standard. Law and medicine have ethical boards of review comprised of fellow professionals. Many times licensing agencies serve as the monitoring mechanism.

For the time being, you will need to be your own monitor of your professional behavior. Consider a model that is used within the religious community for monitoring spiritual life: the use of a spiritual advisor. A spiritual advisor is another person chosen to be a sounding board and to help chart a person's spiritual path. I would like to suggest a parallel person for musicians. Select a person—a colleague, a friend, or even your partner—who can observe you from another point of view and provide an honest and blunt perspective on how your actions are viewed by others. Give this person your code of ethics. In the most ideal of worlds, it would be best if your "ethical advisor" were a colleague, who you in turn could serve as an ethical advisor for—a system of ethical checks and balances of sorts. By doing so, you commit yourself to a code of behavior to which you can be held accountable.

If you feel uncomfortable having an "ethical advisor" for any reason, then I strongly suggest the system used by Weston Noble, which that I wrote about earlier in this text: self-journaling. For this system to work, you must write at the end of each day without fail. Aspects of your life that have fallen short of your ethical code must be written in red. Your role the next day, then, is to correct the things written in red. If you succeed, then write over them in blue to

symbolize a change in your behavior toward others. This system of self-monitoring is perhaps the strongest system any of us could hope for because it is both corrective and prescriptive, and it places total responsibility for our daily actions on ourselves.

In the back of this book, you will find "My Ethical Notebook"—pages for your use in constructing a code of ethics. Consider the guidelines suggested here. But remember that you, your heart, and what you know is right will serve as your final arbiters in this most difficult, but most important, of tasks.

"...our most important life work as musicians is to bring meaning to our life..."

"Sunset IV"

Chapter 27

The End Is the Beginning: Coming Full Circle

The purpose of art is not the release of a momentary ejection of adrenaline but is, rather, the gradual, lifelong construction of a state of wonder and serenity.

Glenn Gould
"Let's Ban Applause"
Musical America (1962)

Jung, for one, takes the opposite view. For him middle-aged man loses contact with unconscious phantasy not because his mental life dries up, but because archetypal images, the symbols of mental rebirth, are again stirring in the depth of his mind; if he fails to respond actively to their challenge, he becomes cut off from his creative unconscious and develops neurosis. (p. 290)

Anton Ehrenzweig
The Hidden Order of Art

334

I am done with great things and big plans, great institutions and big successes. I am for those tiny, invisible loving human forces that work from individual, creeping through the crannies of the world like so many other rootlets, or like the capillary of oozing water, yet which, if given time, will rend the hardest monuments of human pride.

William James

There are times when we must allow some of the unlived life within us to live if we are to get new energies for living.... The important thing, as has been said before but what must be said again for emphasis, is that we recognize the Shadow side of ourselves. This recognition alone produces a powerful and beneficial change in consciousness...everything in the unconscious that has been repressed strives for reunion with consciousness. It is as though we put certain things in the basement of our house and shut the door tightly. But these things do not want to remain in the basement. They turn into devils and rattle the door and seek to find some way out of their imprisoned state and back into the world of consciousness. In so doing, they create anxiety, since we tend to fear the return of the repressed. But this attempt of repressed contents to reach consciousness is not simply an attempt to disturb consciousness or gain revenge. The movement is toward the light of consciousness because this is necessary if psychological redemption is to occur. No matter how malignant these split-off contents of the psyche may appear to be, and no matter how malicious their tricks, there is always the possibility of their redemption if they can reach consciousness. Paradoxically, the redemption of these lost parts of ourselves also results in our redemption. That is, we can be whole only when we have helped redeem our devils.... Wholeness can only emerge when both sides of the coin are represented in consciousness at the same time; when we remain conscious of both our light and dark sides. (pp. 22–23)

John Sanford

Creating the Special World by Weston Noble

There is a story about a young monk who asked the Buddha why he was the Buddha. "Is it because you have mastered all your desires?" "No," was the reply. "Are you the Buddha because you can levitate?" Again, "no" was the answer. "Because you can know all things?" Once again, the simple answer was "no." "Then, why are you called the Buddha, the Enlightened One?" The Buddha's response was, "I am only awake." (p. 22)

Don G. Campbell

The Roar of Silence

336

Man achieves fullness of being in fellowship, in care for others. He expands his existence by "bearing his fellow man's burden." As we have said, animals are concerned for their own needs; the degree of our being human stands in direct proportion to the degree in which we care for others. (p. 47)

The sense of wonder is not the mist in our eyes or the fog in our words. Wonder or radical amazement, is a way of going beyond what is given in thing and thought, refusing to take anything for granted, to regard anything as final. It is our honest response to the grandeur and mystery of reality, our confrontation with that which transcends the given. (p. 79)

Abraham Joshua Heschel

Who Is Man?

So where has the musician's walk brought us? In the course of *The Musician's Soul, The Musician's Spirit,* and *The Musician's Walk,* have we settled any questions? I have likely managed to unearth more questions than I have answered, which was my intent. But I have come to realize that it is perhaps our most important life's work as musicians to bring meaning to our life so that meaning can be reflected in the music we make. Mental anguish is often heaped upon musicians when they feel a certain meaninglessness of being. It is not enough, as Heschel states, to acknowledge and state that "I am," but

337

rather to constantly seek the answer to who "I am" in relation to who we live and make music with on a daily basis. To be human is to care deeply for life's meanings, whether through understanding of one's inner self, through one's life experiences as evidenced in story, or through the lessons learned by human, caring interaction with others.

It seems that for artists, this reduces down to a relatively simple premise. Is it sufficient enough to merely "be" as musicians, or must we spend every waking minute understanding what it is to live? Alive music is music that is significantly different from music that just "is," or that is just in a state of being. Musicians must acknowledge that being *is* the life mystery and seek whatever means to understand it. If we continue to explore our humanness through thought and reflection, we will realize Heschel's concept of the imperative of awe. Music that is created out of some understanding of being becomes an experience not because we will it or desire it to be, but rather because it stuns us at every turn and gives us daily courage to brave the impact of the sublime. If we believe music possesses transcendent meaning, then we must also accept the fact that that meaning surpasses comprehension. Comprehension should not be our goal. Our goal needs to be to understand the mission of being the vehicle, both in life and music. It is our walk that can become our vehicle.

338

Monks, what is the noble truth
About the way that goes into
The cessation of suffering?

Just this noble eightfold way,
Namely, right view, right purpose,
Right speech, right action,
Right livelihood, right effort, right mindfulness,
And right concentration (p. 269)

The Buddha

The Direct Path by Andrew Harvey

By thinking intensely
Of the good of others,
By devoting yourself to their service,
You will purify your heart
By that work and through it
You will arrive at the vision of Self
Which penetrates all living things. (p. 66)

Vivekananda

The Direct Path by Andrew Harvey

My Ethical Notebook

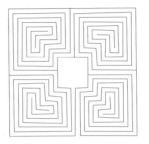

340   *Note ideas taken from readings in this book
that have resonated with you. Refer to any
of your marginal notes, if applicable.*

342 *Write an extended essay about an influential human being in your life.*

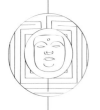

344   *Find a picture of a person or an event in your life that will inspire a good way of being every time you look at it.*

345

346   *Construct a list of ethical rules based upon*
experiences in your life.

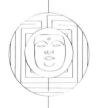

347

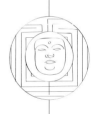

348

My Ethical Rules

Using the lists constructed on the previous pages, develop a list of ethical rules for your own professional and musical conduct. Before writing your list, determine how you will monitor your behavior on a daily basis. Retype your list and post it in several places, such as in your rehearsal folder, framed in your office, etc.

Postscript

Liberal Education Rediscovered

by L. Jackson Newell

We conclude this book with a postscript.

Stepping back from our specific focus on music, the author invited Professor Newell, a historian of higher education, to remind us of the larger aims of a college education—without which no academic or professional major could be fully developed or appreciated. Addressing the entering class at a University of Utah Honors convocation shortly before he accepted the presidency at Deep Springs College in California, Professor Newell urged all freshman to think about the opportunities of their college years in the broadest possible terms. Here's what he had to say....

352

I congratulate each of you for having earned a sought-after place in the university's undergraduate program. Take it seriously, and take it fully, and this faculty and curriculum will transform you in ways that neither you nor we can predict. This statement, of course, may not sit comfortably with you. After all, maybe *you* don't need to be transformed. Or perhaps you think the faculty ought to be more accountable for what happens to you while you study with us? Do I *really* mean that the experience you embark upon today, and this university, will change you in ways we cannot predict?

My purpose is to explore with you what effects (and the word "effects" is emphatically plural here) a good college education should have on students. What are the responsibilities you as students and we as professors bear along the path that we will tread together over the next four years? One of these is to explore, understand, and practice an ideal that is the mutual responsibility of all professors regardless of their disciplines: liberal education. It is the open mind and broad understanding that emanates from this attitude toward learning and life that ultimately underpins and provides context for the practice of every major offered on this campus, from music theory to social work and from chemistry to psychology. A good liberal education, available but not always understood or appreciated, is yours for the taking, though it is often packaged as a set of seemingly unrelated courses called "general education" or labeled "distribution requirements." Chosen wisely and taken seriously, however, these courses can become the source of your human understanding—and, thus, the anchor of your professional ethics.

Each year I teach liberal education courses in the university's honors program as well as in my own program. I like undergraduates in either setting, but I like them for different reasons. Honors students,

353

on the whole, are faster readers, better writers, and more advanced in their aesthetic and academic understanding. But when I compare them with my other students, honors students are often *less* likely to try new ideas or venture out into new territory—for fear of risking a lofty GPA or wounding a well-padded ego.

Problems in American education, however, are hardly attributable to one kind of student or another. Our whole approach to learning leaves much to be desired. A century and a half ago, Emerson lamented that American students "are shut up in school and college recitation rooms for ten or fifteen years and come out at last with a bellyful of words and do not know a thing" (Letter of September 14, 1839). We learn to know with our heads, he said, but not with our hearts and hands. College students today are more likely to have accompanied Tensing and Hillary on the first conquest of Mt. Everest through the pages of a book than to have climbed the highest mountain or promontory in their state. They are more likely to have studied Mother Teresa's ministry to the suffering multitudes in Calcutta than to have helped or even talked with a homeless person in their own town. American students and faculty are especially inclined to judge others, and themselves, by what they have read.

Leroy "Satchel" Paige, the great and seemingly ageless baseball pitcher, spent most of his illustrious career in the old Negro leagues that existed before the National and American Leagues allowed "Blacks" to play ball for them. Shortly after World War II, when he was in his forties, Satchel joined the Cleveland Indians and pitched another ten years. When asked the secret that enabled him to keep his edge as a major leaguer long after his contemporaries had retired, Satchel responded dryly, "Don't look back, something may be gaining on you."

How many times have you looked over your shoulder and gauged *your* progress by who is falling behind or who may be gaining on you? This mentality is nothing less than grading yourself on the curve, and it is dangerous business because your reference for success becomes external and relative rather than internal. Being a college student, I contend, means setting your own objectives and your own standards of excellence—and purposely making room in your academic and personal schedule to explore new ideas and accept new challenges. Courage is always needed to confront disturbing new ideas and information, and it takes fortitude to enroll in a course that you know will require skills you don't yet possess (and fear you never will). But growth always involves risk, and your willingness to venture beyond the safety of your strengths must spring from your interior. I urge you to look inside yourself, not over your shoulder, as you chart your course and measure your progress. But how might you do this?

Let's take a closer look at the map of this territory you enter today. While you won't be the first scholar to explore the region of ideas that will open up to you here, there are real frontiers out there, and you may be the first to set eye or foot upon one of them. You may wish to think of your adventure as distinctly twofold, for you will not only be expanding your knowledge and skills through your outward venture into the physical world and into the tangible realms of music, geology, history, or anthropology (to pick just four disciplines as examples), but like any traveler or explorer, you can expect to learn as much about *yourself* as you do about the terrain. This dimension of your journey is an inward one, and the landscape is made up of the feelings, thoughts, and values that are inspired by your experiences. I am talking about your *responses* to what you discover and the *meaning* you choose to attach to your growing knowledge.

Your responses to what you learn may be subjective, and they will certainly be personal, but they are no less important than the mathematical formulas, scientific theories, or enduring works of art or literature that you study. Why? Because your values will ultimately guide your perceptions of truth, your use of knowledge, your application of hard-won skills. "Education," Socrates reputedly said, "must focus its main efforts on thinking about and examining our beliefs, studying them not as if they were alien objects, but rather from within, the beliefs as well as their study being seen as an integral part of the serious drama in which we are involved." In our own century, essayist and theologian Thomas Merton asserted that education consists of "learning who one is, and what one has to offer the contemporary world, and how to make that offering valid." When we think of education in these terms, it becomes quite clear why looking over your shoulder is bad business and why predicting the outcomes of education is impossible.

We faculty are here as guides to lead you into the finest texts and most enduring ideas, music, and art that we ourselves have come to know. And if we have a little of Emerson in our marrow, we will also go beyond the university's gates with you to observe and, where possible, take part in the social, cultural, and natural environments around us. Beyond the camaraderie engendered by these common experiences, however, your journey will also have an important solitary dimension. *You* must decide how earnestly you will strive to understand each new idea, and if you accept it, you alone can decide what claim it has on your actions. Will justice, beauty, or mercy remain abstract terms to you, or will you plumb their depths and give life to these noble concepts in your dealings with others? You decide how you will live. Despite Socrates' and Merton's admonitions, and the best efforts of many able faculty, universities seldom give your inward excursion—your quest to forge a philosophy of life—its due. There are reasons for this imbalance, and some of them are good reasons. Let me explain.

356

While we can and should acknowledge and support each other's inward quest, we can't share it as fully as we share the texts, theories, and matter that are typically the objects of our study. Universities are sometimes called the "household of reason." Reason, based on sensory observations, is the chief method of the external search—it is our means of making sense of the objects and processes we encounter around us. We like to think of observation and reason as being objective because we yearn for clarity and, by nature, want to be sure about things. Ambiguity gives us the willies. In academic discourse, we *generally* confine our attention to matters that we can observe (directly or indirectly) and to claims that we can verify with evidence that reasonable people might consider seriously. The external quest, then, usually seeks to identify and understand what is in our universe—including ourselves—and how it all works. It is concerned primarily with what is rather than with what ought to be; it deals more with physical than with metaphysical questions. This quest is "external" in the sense that we depend upon commonly accepted standards and verifiable evidence to support our conjectures and conclusions.

But can our scientific and aesthetic conclusions really be objective? Try as we may, our creative work and scholarship seldom meet that lofty standard. On the one hand, we may not always focus on the most important elements in a situation, and when we do, the instruments we employ to aid our senses are sometimes flawed, as is our ability to organize and make sense of the torrent of information we (with our instruments, questionnaires, and the like) may gather. More importantly, what we "see" and, therefore, what we report to one another is influenced substantially by what we assume to be true or hope to find. Sooner or later we must each reckon with the wisdom of this ironic twist of a common phrase: "If I hadn't believed it, I wouldn't have seen it!"

357

We have come full circle. As we now set out together to explore and further map the terrain of the physical universe we inhabit and the social and artistic worlds we have constructed, it is clear that we must proceed with humility sufficient to recognize the inherent subjectivity of our observations and knowledge—as well as the subjectivity of our own experience and interpretations. It is vitally important, therefore, that you examine your beliefs and values consciously and candidly, because they will exert a powerful influence not only on how you will live and what you will become, but also on how you will learn and what you will know.

I began by urging you to take your internal journey as seriously as the external one. Now I argue that the two are inseparably linked. Your task is to see and understand the ties between these two passages and to forge strong connections between what you learn and how you will live.

How might we more fully link our needs for knowing and valuing, and keep these two objectives equally vital? Our best hope is to create and maintain within the university a climate of intellectual and moral freedom that affords each student and professor the opportunity to fully develop and express her or his own thoughts and beliefs. The quality of our individual thoughts and the integrity of our personal beliefs depend not on their conformity with prevailing opinions, but on their ability to weather encounters with new information, competing ideas, and contrasting values.

We cannot learn to think well without the freedom to be, simply and authentically, ourselves. We cannot become what we seek to be without occasionally risking embarrassment or failure. Thinking freely and risking judgment—these qualities may be encouraged or (more often) suppressed by the groups within which we live and

358

work. We can claim them for ourselves if we are strong enough or perhaps callous enough, but most of us need the support of one another and we thrive best in an environment of mutual respect.

Academic freedom is our most fundamental value in higher education, but I have taught too long to have any illusions about students' experiences. Few believe they can differ with a professor and still be graded fairly. In most cases, these perceptions are mistaken or amplified, but just enough exceptions occur to keep students' fears alive. Suffice to say, we must recommit ourselves—faculty and students alike—to protect our right to free inquiry and our responsibility to pursue truth and beauty wherever they may lead us. Without academic freedom, we cannot properly pursue our creative and scholarly objectives or be about the important work of defining and refining our personal and social values. We must welcome in this academy alternate interpretations of present realities and encourage the expression of a rich variety of personal beliefs about what is desirable for us and for our local, national, and global communities. By looking candidly at "what is" and considering contrasting views of "what might be," we open the door to the most distinctively human of all activities: thinking and acting to improve the human condition, including our own condition.

The aim of liberal education, pioneering psychologist Abraham Maslow believed, is to create a "fully functioning human being." Such a person is alive in all the dimensions that make us human, being intellectually active and curious, emotionally aware and sensitive, spiritually resonate in the highest sense, and physically robust within our natural or imposed limits. According to Maslow, fully functioning people—healthy people—bring a matter-of-fact approach to the world while living with uncommon delight. They simply accept human nature for what it is, and seek to understand it. But they also strive, instinctively it seems, to bring some mercy and justice into their

communities—harboring neither unrealistic hopes nor feelings of
futility about their prospects for success. They know what they value,
and they do what they feel they must do.

Knowing. Valuing. Doing. Linking these ideals is the aim of a
college education. Set your own goals, establish lofty standards for
yourself, and offer what you have to offer the contemporary world.
And may *you* study and live with uncommon delight.

L. Jackson Newell

Throughout his career, Professor Newell has devoted himself to
the improvement of undergraduate education and the teaching of
ethics, believing that the anemic notion of liberal education now in
vogue is selling students short and leaving faculty without a broad
educational vision. Now Scholar-in-Residence with the Utah Board of
Regents, Newell is University Professor Emeritus at the University of
Utah and President Emeritus at Deep Springs College. He won the
Joseph Katz Award for his distinctive contributions to the
advancement of liberal learning in America.

"That was a memorable day for me..."

"Flor

That was a memorable day for me,

for it made great changes in me,

But, it is the same way with any life.

Imagine one selected day struck out of it,

and think how different its course would have been.

Pause you who read this, and think for a moment

of the long chain of iron or gold,

of thorns or flowers,

that would never have bound you,

but for the formation of the first link

on one memorable day.

Charles Dickens

"Tomorrow is a new day."

"Vista I"

363

You must learn from the mistakes of others. You can't possibly live
long enough to make them all yourself.

                                              Sam Levenson

Finish each day and be done with it.
You have done what you could.
Some blunders and absurdities have crept in;
forget them as soon as you can.
Tomorrow is a new day;
you shall begin it serenely and with too high a spirit
to be encumbered with your old nonsense.

                                      Ralph Waldo Emerson

When one door of happiness closes, another opens;
but often we look so long at the closed door
that we do not see the one which has been opened for us.

                                              Helen Keller

"I don't develop, I am." —Pablo Picasso

"Sunset Three"

We grow accustomed to the Dark—
When light is put away—
And when the Neighbor holds the Lamp
To witness her Goodbye—

A Moment—We uncertain step
For newness of the night—
Then—fit our Vision to the Dark—
And meet the Road—erect—

And so of larger—Darknesses—
Those Evenings of the Brain—
When not a Moon disclose a sign—
Or star—come out—within—

The Bravest—grope a little—
And sometimes hit a Tree
Directly in the Forehead—
But as they learn to see—

Either the darkness alters—
Or something in the sight
Adjusts itself to Midnight—
And Life steps almost straight.

Emily Dickinson

Many people will walk in and out of your life, but only true friends will leave footprints in your heart.

To handle yourself, use your head; to handle others, use your heart. Anger is only one letter short of danger.

If someone betrays you once, it is his fault; if he betrays you twice, it is your fault.

Great minds discuss ideas; average minds discuss events; small minds discuss people.

If you lose money, you lose much; if you lose friends, you lose more; if you lose faith, you lose all.

Beautiful young people are accidents of nature, but beautiful old people are works of art.

Friends, you and me...you brought another friend....and then there were three...we started our group...our circle of friends...and like that circle...there is no beginning or end.

Yesterday is history, tomorrow is mystery, today is a gift, that's why they call it the present.

Eleanor Roosevelt

The aim of life is to live,
And to live means to be aware, joyously, drunkenly, serenely,
divinely aware.

Henry Miller

"...be aware..."

"Yin"

"...the final part of the musician's journey."

"Shadow

Bibliography and Suggested Reading

Artress, Lauren. *Walking a Sacred Path: Rediscovering the Labyrinth as a Spiritual Tool.* New York: Riverhead Books, 1995.

Barenboim, Daniel, and Edward W. Said. *Parallels and Paradoxes: Explorations in Music and Society.* New York: Pantheon Books, 2002.

Barzon, J. "The Paradoxes of Creativity," *The American Scholar,* No. 50. Summer 1989, pp. 337–51.

Becker, Ernest. *The Denial of Death.* New York: Simon and Schuster, 1973.

Bell, John L. *States of Bliss and Yearning: The Marks and Means of Authentic Christian Spirituality.* Chicago: GIA Publications, Inc., 2002.

Bennett-Goleman, Tara. *Emotional Alchemy: How the Mind Can Heal the Heart.* New York: Harmony Books, 2001.

Blackburn, Simon. *Truth: A Guide.* London: Oxford University Press, 2005.

Blitt, Rita. *The Passionate Gesture.* Brandeis University: RAM Publications, 2000.

Blocker, Robert, ed. *The Robert Shaw Reader.* New Haven, CT: Yale University Press, 2004.

Bloom, Harold. *Where Shall Wisdom Be Found?* New York: Riverhead Books, 2004.

Bonhoeffer, Dietrich. *Ethics.* New York: SCM Press, Ltd., 1955.

370 ——. Eberhard Bethge, ed. *Letters and Papers from Prison.* New York: SCM Press, Ltd., 1971.

Bonnici, John S. *Person to Person: Friendship and Love in the Life and Theology of Hans Urs von Balthasar.* New York: Alba House, 1999.

Boring, Edwin G. *Sensation and Perception in the History of Experimental Psychology.* New York: Irvington Publishers, Inc., 1977.

Boyce, Barry. "Two Sciences of the Mind." *Shambala Sun.* November 2004.

Briehl, Susan, and Marty Haugen. *Turn My Heart: A Sacred Journey from Brokenness to Healing.* Chicago: GIA Publications, Inc., 2004.

Briggs, John. *Fractals: The Patterns of Chaos.* New York: Simon and Schuster, 1992.

Brodie, Renee. *The Healing Tones of Crystal Bowls.* Vancouver, Canada: Aroma Art Limited, 1996.

Bunch, Meribeth. "Are You All There?" *The Strad.* August 2002.

Bunge, Wilfred F. *Warmly, Weston: A Luther College Life.* Decorah, IA: Luther College Press, 1998.

Campbell, Don G. *The Roar of Silence: Healing Powers of Breath, Tone and Music.* Wheaton, IL: Theosophical Publishing House, 1989.

Cameron, Julia. *Inspirations.* New York: Penguin Putnam, Inc., 2001.

——.*The Sound of Paper: Starting from Scratch.* New York: Tarcher/Penguin Books, 2004.
> *This book is highly recommended by the author. Julia Cameron sets out many approaches and formats of journaling. As with all her other books, it is not only informative but also inspirational.*

——.*Walking in This World.* New York: Penguin Putnam, Inc., 2002.

Chodron, Pema. *Start Where You Are: A Guide to Compassionate Living.* Boston, MA: Shambhala, 2001.

——.*When Things Fall Apart: Heart Advice for Difficult Times.* Boston, MA: Shambhala, 2000.

Coffin, William Sloane. *A Passion for the Possible: A Message to U.S. Churches.* Louisville, KY: Westminster/John Knox Press, 1993.

——.*Credo.* Louisville, KY: Westminster/John Knox Press, 2004.

——.*The Heart Is a Little to the Left.* Hannover, NH: University Press of New England, 1999.

Connor, Danny. *QiGong: Chinese Movement and Meditation for Health* (featuring Master Michael Tse). Boston, MA: Red Wheel/Weiser, LLC, 1992.

Crowe, Barbara. *Music and Soul Making: Toward a New Theory of Music Therapy.* Toronto, Canada: Scarecrow Press, 2004.

Cutting, Linda Katherine. *Memory Slips: A Memoir of Music and Healing.* New York: HarperCollins Publishers, 1997.

Dalai Lama, The, and Victor Chan. *The Wisdom of Forgiveness: Intimate Conversations and Journeys.* New York: Riverhead Books, 2004.

Dalai Lama, The. *Ethics for the New Millennium: His Holiness The Dalai Lama.* New York: Riverhead Books, 2001.

Damasio, Antonio. *Descartes' Error: Emotion, Reason, and the Human Brain.* New York: HarperCollins Publishers, 2000.

——. *Looking for Spinoza: Joy, Sorrow, and the Feeling Brain.* New York: Harcourt, Inc., 2003.

——. *The Feeling of What Happens.* New York: Harcourt, Inc., 1999.

da Silva, Kim. *Gesundheit in unseren Handen.* Munich, Germany: Droemersche Verlagsanstalt Th. Knaur Nachf, 2000.

372

De Mello, Anthony. *Awareness: The Perils and Opportunities of Reality.* New York: Doubleday, 1990.

Dewey, John. *Art As Experience.* New York: The Berkley Publishing Group, 1980.

Diamond, John. *Behavioral Kinesiology.* New York: HarperCollins Publishers, 1979.

Dowrick, Stephanie. *Intimacy and Solitude: Balancing Closeness and Independence.* New York: W. W. Norton & Company, 1991.

Ehrenzweig, Anton. *The Hidden Order of Art: A Study in the Psychology of Artistic Imagination.* Berkeley, CA: University of California Press, 1967.

Eldredge, John. *Waking the Dead: The Glory of a Heart Fully Alive.* Nashville, TN: Thomas Nelson, Inc., 2003.

Emerson, Ralph Waldo. Joel Myerson, ed. *The Selected Letters of Ralph Waldo Emerson.* New York: Columbia University Press, 1997.

Fogelin, Robert. *Walking the Tightrope of Reason: The Precarious Life of a Rational Animal.* London: Oxford University Press, 2003.

Frankfurt, Harry G. *The Reasons of Love.* Princeton, NJ: Princeton University Press, 2004.

Fromm, Erich. *The Art of Loving.* New York: HarperCollins Publishers, 2000.

Gafni, Marc. *Soul Prints.* New York: Simon and Schuster, 2001.

Gandhi, Mahatma. Kripalani, Krishna, ed. *All Men Are Brothers: Autobiographical Reflections.* New York: Continuum Press, 1999.

Gardner, Howard. *Changing Minds: The Art and Science of Changing Our Own and Other People's Minds.* Boston, MA: Harvard Business School Press, 2004.

Gazzaniga, Michael, *The Ethical Brain.* Chicago: University of Chicago Press, 2005.

Gladwell, Malcolm. *Blink: The Power of Thinking Without Thinking*. New York: Little, Brown and Company, 2005.
> *This fascinating book should be read by every ensemble conductor. Reading the book brings an awareness of how we make many decisions in an instant. This instantaneous decision making about people and music making can be an asset or a hindrance to musicians.*

Goldman, Jonathan. *Healing Sounds: The Power of Harmonics*. Rochester, VT: Healing Arts Press, 2002.

Goldman, Jonathan, and Andi Goldman. *Tantra of Sound: How to Enhance Intimacy with Sound*. Charlottesville, VA: Hampton Roads Publishing Company, 2005.

Goleman, Daniel. *Destructive Emotions: How Can We Overcome Them?* New York: Bantam Dell, 2003.

Gomes, Peter J. *The Good Life: Truths That Last in Times of Need*. San Francisco, CA: HarperCollins Publishers, 2002.

——. *Sermons: Biblical Wisdom for Daily Living*. New York: William Morrow and Company, 1998.

——. *Strength for the Journey: Biblical Wisdom for Daily Living*. San Francisco, CA: HarperCollins Publishers, 2003.

Gracian, Baltasar. Christopher Maurer, trans. *The Art of Wordly Wisdom*. New York: Doubleday, 1992.

Graham, Jorie. *Materialism*. Hopewell, NJ: Ecco Press, 1995.

Green, Barry. *The Mastery of Music: Ten Pathways to True Artistry*. New York: Broadway Books, 2003.

Gyatso, Tenzin (The Fourteenth Dalai Lama). *The Compassionate Life*. Boston, MA: Wisdom Publications, Inc., 2001.

——. *Ethics for the New Millennium* (video). Mystic Fire Video (MYS76497), 2003.

374 Harvey, Andrew. *The Direct Path: Creating a Personal Journey to the Divine Using the World's Spiritual Traditions.* New York: Broadway Books, 2000.

> *This book should be required reading for all musicians. Reading this will give a concise overview of the philosophical and spiritual core of all the world's religions. Harvey offers practical solutions for meditation according to the world's religions.*

——. *The Essential Mystics: The Soul's Journey into Truth.* Edison, NJ: Castle Books, 1998.

Havel, Václav. *Letters to Olga: June 1979–September 1982.* New York: H. Holt, 1989.

Hawkins, David R. *A Map of Consciousness* (video). Sedona, AZ: Institute for Advanced Theoretical Research, 1993.

——. *The Eye of the I.* Sedona, AZ: Veritas Publishing, 2001.

——. *Power vs. Force: The Hidden Determinants of Human Behavior.* Carlsbad, CA: Hay House, Inc., 2002.

Hecht, Jennifer Michael. *Doubt: A History.* San Francisco, CA: HarperCollins Publishers, 2003.

Helmholtz, Hermann von. *Treatise on Physiological Optics.* New York: The Optical Society of America, 1925.

Hendra, Tony. *Father Joe: The Man Who Saved My Soul.* New York: Random House, 2004.

Henri, Robert. *The Art Spirit.* Boulder, CO: Westview Press, 1984.

Heschel, Abraham Joshua. *Between God and Man: An Interpretation of Judaism.* New York: Free Press Paperbacks, 1959.

——. *Moral Grandeur and Spiritual Audacity.* New York: Farrar, Straus and Giroux, 1996.

——. *Who Is Man?* Stanford, CA: Stanford University Press, 1965.

Hillman, James. *Kinds of Power: A Guide to Its Intelligent Uses.* New York: Doubleday, 1995.

——. *Re-Visioning Psychology*. New York: Harper & Row, 1976. **375**

Hirschi, Gertrud. *Mudras: Yoga in Your Hands*. Boston, MA: Weiser Books, 2000.

Holt, Jim. "Of Two Minds." *The New York Times Magazine*. May 8, 2005: pp. 11–3.

Holy Transfiguration Monastery. *The Ascetical Homilies of Saint Isaac the Syrian*. Boston, MA: Holy Transfiguration Monastery, 1984.

Hou, Faxiang, and Mark V. Wiley. *QiGong for Health and Well-Being*. Boston, MA: Journey Editions, 1999.

Isaacson, Walter. *Benjamin Franklin: An American Life*. New York: Simon & Schuster, 2003.

Jansen, Eva Rudy. *Singing Bowls*. Boston, MA: Weiser Books, 1990.

Jordan, James. *Evoking Sound*. Chicago: GIA Publications, Inc., 1996.

——. *Learn Conducting Technique with the Swiss Exercise Ball*. Chicago: GIA Publications, Inc.

——. *The Musician's Soul*. Chicago: GIA Publications, 1999.

——. *The Musician's Spirit*. Chicago: GIA Publications, 2002.

Kennedy, Maxwell Taylor. *Make Gentle the Life of This World*. New York: Broadway Books, 1998.

Koch, Christof. *The Quest for Consciousness: A Neurobiological Approach*. Englewood, CO: Roberts and Company Publishers, 2004.

Kornfield, Jack. *A Path with Heart: A Guide Through the Perils and Promises of Spiritual Life*. New York: Bantam Books, 1993.

Land, George, and Beth Jarman. *Breakpoint and Beyond: Mastering the Future Today*. New York: HarperCollins Publishers, 1992.

376

Lannom, Allen. "A Discarding of Meaningless and Self-Centered Inhibitions." *The Choral Journal.* February 1993, p. 54.

Langer, Ellen J. *The Power of Mindful Learning.* Cambridge, MA: Perseus Publishing, 1997.

Lautzenheiser, Tim. *Music Advocacy and Student Leadership: Key Components of Every Successful Music Program.* Chicago: GIA Publications, 2005.

Lesser, Elizabeth. *The New American Spirituality: A Seeker's Guide.* New York: Random House, 1999.

Liu, Hong. *The Healing Art of QiGong.* New York: Warner Books, 1997.

Loori, John Daido. *The Heart of Being: Moral and Ethical Teachings of Zen Buddhism.* Boston, MA: Charles E. Tuttle Co., 1996.

Marty, Martin E. *A Cry of Absence: Reflections for the Winter of the Heart.* Grand Rapids, MI: Eerdmans Publishing Company, 1997.

Marty, Martin, and Micah Marty. *Places Along the Way: Meditations on the Journey of Faith.* Minneapolis, MN: Augsburg Fortress, 1994.

Maslow, Abraham. H. *The Farther Reaches of Human Nature.* New York: The Viking Press, 1971.

McCormick, Adele von Rust, Deborah Marlena McCormick, and Thomas E. McCormick. *Horses and the Mystical Path: The Celtic Way of Expanding the Human Soul.* Novato, CA: New World Library, 2004.

Merleau-Ponty, Maurice. *Phenomenology of Perception.* New York: Routledge & Kegan Paul, 1962.

Merton, Thomas. *Learning to Love: Exploring Solitude and Freedom.* San Francisco, CA: HarperCollins Publishers, 1977

———. Naomi Burton Stone and Brother Patrick Hart, eds. *Love and Learning.* New York: Harcourt Brace Jovanovich, 1985.

——. *Thoughts in Solitude.* Boston, MA: Shambhala, 1993.

——. *When the Trees Say Nothing: Writings on Nature.* Notre Dame, IN: Sorin Books, 2003.

Moore, Thomas. *Dark Nights of the Soul: A Guide to Finding Your Way through Life's Ordeals.* New York: Gotham Books, 2004.

——. *The Original Self: Living with Paradox and Originality.* New York: HarperCollins Publishers, 2000.

——. *The Soul's Religion: Cultivating a Profoundly Spiritual Way of Life.* New York: HarperCollins Publishers, 2002.

Mussulman, Joseph A. *Dear People...* Chapel Hill, NC: Hinshaw Music, Inc., 1996.

Myss, Caroline. *Why People Don't Heal and How They Can.* New York: Three Rivers Press, 1997.

Namikoshi, Tokojuro. *Japanese Finger Therapy.* New York: Japan Publications, 1994.

Neumann, Erich. *Depth Psychology and a New Ethic.* Boston, MA: Shambhala, 1990.

Newell, L. Jackson. *The Students of Deep Springs College.* Revere, PA: Lodima Press, 2000.

Nhat Hanh, Thich. *Interbeing.* Berkeley, CA: Parallax Press, 1993.

Nhat Hanh, Thich. *Taming the Tiger Within: Meditations on Transforming Difficult Emotions.* New York: Riverhead Books, 2004.

Nietzche, Friedrich. *Human, All-Too-Human.* Lincoln, NE: University of Nebraska Press, 1986.

Noble, Weston. *Creating the Special World: A Collection of Lectures by Weston H. Noble.* Chicago: GIA Publications, 2005.
    This small book is a must read for all choral musicians. While not long, its content is concise and profound. Conductors should study the first three lectures on spirituality.

378   Oliver, Mary. "Low Tide." *Amicus Journal*. Winter 2001.

Osho. *Awareness: The Key to Living in Balance*. New York: St. Martin's Press, 2001.

Palmer, Parker J. *A Hidden Wholeness: The Journey Toward an Undivided Life*. San Francisco, CA: Jossey-Bass, 2004.
   This new book by Parker Palmer is an in-depth study of issues related to ethics of self. The author strongly encourages all readers to study it.

Penderecki, Krzysztof. *Labyrinth of Time*. Chapel Hill, NC: Hinshaw Music, 1998.

Peters, Tom, and Nancy Austin. *A Passion for Excellence: The Leadership Difference*. New York: Warner Books, 1985.

Polisi, Joseph W. *The Artist as Citizen*. Pompton Plains, NJ: Amadeus Press, 2005.

Putnam, Hilary. *Ethics without Ontology*. Cambridge, MA: Harvard University Press, 2004.

Raessler, Kenneth R. *Aspiring to Excel*. Chicago: GIA Publications, 2003.

Rilling, Helmut. *Lectures at the Oregon Bach Festival*. Dayton, OH: The Lorenz Corporation, 2000.

Roberts, Elizabeth, and Elias Amidon. *Life Prayers*. San Francisco, CA: HarperCollins Publishers, 1996.

Rogers, Fred. *The World According to Mister Rogers: Important Things to Remember*. New York: Hyperion, 2003.

Rothko, Mark. *The Artist's Reality: Philosophies of Art*. New Haven, CT: Yale University Press, 2004.

Sacks, Kenneth S. *Understanding Emerson*. Princeton, NJ: Princeton University Press, 2003.

Sahakian, W.S. *History of Psychology*. Itasca, IL: Peacock Publishers, 1980.

Sands, Helen Raphael. *The Healing Labyrinth: Finding Your Path to Inner Peace.* Hauppauge, NY: Barron's Educational Series, Inc., 2001.

Sanford, John. *Evil: The Shadow Side of Reality.* New York: Crossroad Publishing Company, 1981, 1991.

Schafer, Donna. *Labyrinths from the Outside In.* Woodstock, VT: Skylight Paths, 2000.

Shahn, Ben. *The Shape of Content. The Charles Elliot Norton Lectures of 1956–57.* Cambridge, MA: Harvard University Press, 1957.

Sheldrake, R. *A New Science of Life.* London: Victoria Works, 1981.

Smith, Huston. *The Way Things Are.* Berkeley, CA: University of California Press, 2003.

Somerset Maugham. *The Moon and Sixpence.* New York: Penguin Books, 1944.

Standley, Loretta J. *And Who Are You? A Daily Regimen for the Soul.* Bloomington, IN: AuthorHouse, 2003.

Starr, Mirabai. *The Interior Castle: St. Teresa of Avila.* New York: Riverhead Books, 2003.

Tharp, Twyla. *The Creative Habit: Learn to Use It for Life.* New York: Simon & Schuster, 2003.

Thondup, Tulku. *The Healing Power of the Mind.* Boston, MA: Shambhala, 1998.

Thurman, Robert A. F. *A Simple Monk.* Novato, CA: New World Library, 2003.

Todd, Mabel E. *The Thinking Body: A Study of the Balancing Forces of Dynamic Man.* Pennington, NJ: Princeton Book Company, 1937.

Tzu, Lao. Ralph Alan Dale, trans. *Tao Te Ching.* New York: Barnes and Noble Books, 2002.

380

Van Dyke, Deborah. *Travelling the Sacred Sound Current: Keys for Conscious Evolution.* Bowen Island, BC, Canada: Sound Current Music, 2001.

Walsh, M., ed. *Butler's Lives of the Saints.* New York: Harper and Row, 1985.

Walther, D. *Applied Kinesiology.* Pueblo, CO: Systems D C, 1976.

Wei, Ou Wen. *Pan Gu Mystical QiGong.* Burbank, CA: Multi-Media Books, 1999.

West, Melissa Gayle. *Exploring the Labyrinth.* New York: Broadway Books, 2000.

Westbury, Virginia. *Labyrinths: Ancient Paths of Wisdom and Peace.* New York: Da Capo Press, 2001.

Whitman, Walt. *Leaves of Grass and Other Writings.* New York: W. W. Norton & Company, 2002.

Whitmyer, Claude. *Mindfulness and Meaningful Work:Explorations in Right Livelihood.* Berkeley, CA: Parallax Press, 1994.

Whyte, David. *Crossing the Unknown Sea: Work as a Pilgrimage of Identity.* New York: Berkeley Publishing Group, 2001.

Wilber, Ken, ed. *The Holographic Paradigm and Other Paradoxes.* Boston, MA: Shambhala, 1982.

Wing, R. *The Tao of Power.* Garden City, NY: Doubleday, 1986.

Wolfe, Alan. *The Transformation of American Religion.* New York: Free Press, 2003.

Wordsworth, William. From lines composed a few miles above Tintern Abbey, on revisiting the banks of the Wye during a tour. July 13, 1798.

Wright, Craig. *The Maze and the Warrior: Symbols in Architecture, Theology and Music.* Cambridge, MA: Harvard University Press, 2001.
This is a fascinating book on the history of the labyrinth. This book is highly recommended to those who desire a comprehensive look into the history and uses of the labyrinth.

Yang, Jwing-Ming. *The Root of Chinese QiGong: Secrets for Health, Longevity, and Enlightenment.* Roslindale, MA: YMAA Publications, 1997.

Yang, Jwing-Ming. *QiGong Meditation: Embryonic Breath.* Boston, MA: YMAA Publications, 2003.

Zaleski, Philip. *The Best American Spiritual Writing of 2004.* Boston, MA: Houghton-Mifflin, 2004.

Zander, Rosamund Stone, and Benjamin Zander. *The Art of Possibility: Transforming Professional and Personal Life.* Boston, MA: Harvard Business School Press, 2000.

Videos

Yang, Jwing-Ming. *Eight Simple QiGong Exercises.* Roslindale, MA: YMAA Publications, 2003.
> This video is a complete self-instructional course in QiGong exercises. In addition to exercises, the video contains background information on QiGong and in-depth discussions of the practice.

Web Sites

Grace Cathedral, San Francisco:
www.gracecathedral.org

Grace Cathedral, Worldwide Labyrinth Project:
www.gracecathedral.org

Georgetown University, labyrinth resource:
www.georgetown.edu/labyrinth

Labyrinth Company, manufacturer of various types of labyrinths:
www.labyrinthcompany.com

Labyrinth Society:
www.labyrinthsociety.org

Reiki Master and Sound Healer Astarius:
www.astarius.com
> Many recordings are listed on this site.

"Floral Composition

About the Author and Contributors

james jordan

James Jordan is recognized and praised from many quarters in the musical world as one of the nation's preeminent conductors, writers, and innovators in choral music. Having been called a "visionary" by *The Choral Journal,* his career and publications have been devoted to innovative educational changes in the choral art that have been embraced around the world. A master teacher, Dr. Jordan's pioneering writing and research concerning the use of Laban Movement Analysis for the teaching of conducting and movement to children has dramatically changed teaching in both of those disciplines. Called the "Father of the Case Study," he was the first researcher to bring forward the idea of the case study as a viable and valuable form of research for the training and education of teachers.

One of the country's most prolific writers on the subjects of the philosophy of music making and choral teaching, Dr. Jordan has produced ten major textbooks and several choral series bearing his name, and he has contributed to four other textbooks. In addition to this book, three new books authored by Dr. Jordan were published in 2004: *Learn Conducting Technique with the Swiss Exercise Ball, Ear Training Immersion Exercises for Choirs* (Conductor's Edition with CD and Singer's Edition), and *The Choral Warm-Up* (book with CD and Accompanist Supplement) (all published with GIA Publications, Chicago). His books on the subject of Vocal Technique for Choirs are considered as essential for the education of conductors around the world. His choral conducting book, *Evoking Sound,* was named on a "must read" list of six books by *The Choral Journal.* His *Ear Training Immersion Exercises for Choirs* details the first comprehensive approach toward aural literacy for choirs using a method called

384 "Harmonic Immersion Solfege," which uses a unique system of score analysis that focuses on what is aurally perceived by the choir. His books, *The Musician's Soul* (GIA, 1999) and *The Musician's Spirit* (GIA, 2002), acclaimed by both instrumental and choral conductors alike, have been credited with beginning a transformation on how music is taught both in ensembles and in the classroom through a process of humanizing and loving. His latest text for conductors, *The Choral Conductor's Aural Tutor* (GIA, 2005), is the first text of its kind designed to train conductors to hear and diagnose vocal issues within a choir.

Dr. Jordan also serves as Executive Editor of the *Evoking Sound Choral Series,* published by GIA Publications in Chicago. This series presents choral literature at the highest levels for high school and college choirs. In addition to new compositions by America's finest composers, the series also presents new editions of standard choral repertoire, edited with singers in mind. Also unique to this series are solfege editions that apply Jordan's groundbreaking approach to the use of Harmonic Immersion Solfege in choral ensembles, utilizing accurate aural analysis as the basis of the approach.

Dr. Jordan teaches and conducts at Westminster Choir College of Rider University in Princeton, New Jersey, one of the foremost centers for the study and performance of choral music in the world. At Westminster, he is an Associate Professor of Conducting and a Senior Conductor. For the past twelve years, he has served as conductor of The Westminster Chapel Choir. In the fall of 2004, he became the founding conductor of one of Westminster's highly select touring choirs, a newly inaugurated ensemble, The Westminster Williamson Voices. This choir's mission is not only choral performance and recording at the highest levels, but to serve as an ensemble that employs unique and cutting-edge approaches to choral rehearsal and choral performance. The ensemble has at its center a significant outreach to the musical world through workshops and residencies. The ensemble specializes in premiering significant contributions to the choral literature. The Westminster Williamson Voices ensemble is also involved in educational recordings of significant educational choral literature for the next five years with GIA Publications, which will culminate in the recording of approximately one hundred essential pieces of choral literature. The first in a series of those recordings is scheduled for release by GIA in December of 2005.

Since 2004, Dr. Jordan has served as Visiting Distinguished Professor of Music Education at West Chester University in West Chester, Pennsylvania. He is also on the faculty of the Samuel Barber Summer Institute at West Chester University.

James Jordan has been the recipient of many awards for his contributions to the profession. He was named Distinguished Choral Scholar at The University of Alberta. He was made an honorary member of Phi Mu Alpha Sinfonia in 2002 at Florida State University. Composer Morten Lauridsen dedicated a movement of his acclaimed *Mid-Winter Songs* to Dr. Jordan.

This year alone, Dr. Jordan will present over thirty keynote addresses and workshops around the world. Dr. Jordan's book and professional activities are detailed on his Web site at *www.Evokingsound.com*, and also at *www.giamusic.com*, the Web site of GIA Publications.

photographs

eric scott kephart

Eric Scott Kephart is a graduate of the Art Institute of Philadelphia. His career encompasses many diverse artistic interests, from fashion design to painting, photography, graphic design, and various genres of performance art. He is the owner/curator of ZONK ARTS Gallery in Philadelphia, which specializes in the showcasing and promotion of emerging artists and has a significant community outreach to support artists in Philadelphia. As an artist, Mr. Kephart's current interests include modern pointillism. In addition to *The Musician's Walk,* his photography can be seen in one of Jordan's other books, *The Musician's Spirit.* Mr. Kephart is active in The Philadelphia Art Community through his volunteer work for such outreach organizations as Journey Home, Long Live the Arts Benefit for the South Street Renaissance Gallery, and ASIAC (Aids Services in the Asian Community). His work can be seen on his Web site: *www.zonkarts.com.*

brother emmanuel morinelli, o.c.s.o.

A native of Philadelphia, Br. Emmanuel Morinelli is both a visual artist and a musician. He attended the Philadelphia College of Art and the Catholic University of America in Washington, DC, where he earned his B.A. and M.F.A. in Studio Art. He also holds an M.A. in Music, with a concentration in Church Music and Liturgy, from Saint Joseph's College in Rensselaer, Indiana. In 1983, he entered Saint Joseph's Abbey in Spencer, Massachusetts, where he currently serves as choir director and organist.

contributing authors

james abbington

James Abbington, currently a professor of music in the Department of Fine Arts at Morgan State University, comes to Baltimore from Raleigh, North Carolina, where he was Associate Professor of Music and Chair of the Department of Visual and Performing Arts at Shaw University (1998–2003). He is also Executive Editor of the African American Church Music Series, published by GIA Publications, Inc. in Chicago, and has served as co-director of the annual Hampton University Ministers' and Musicians' Conference since 2000.

Dr. Abbington is a member of the Executive Committee of the Hymn Society in the United States and Canada, as well as a member of the Council for the Calvin Institute for Christian Worship. He proudly serves on Council for the journal *Reformed Worship* (Calvin Institute) and on the advisory board of *African American Pulpit,* a homiletic journal.

Dr. Abbington is a graduate of Morehouse College in Atlanta, Georgia, where he received his Bachelor of Arts in Music and was a student of the late Dr. Wendell P. Whalum and Dr. Joyce Finch Johnson. He earned his Master of Music and Doctor of Musical Arts in Church Music and Organ from the University of Michigan at Ann Arbor, where he was a student of Marilyn Mason.

Dr. Abbington served as Minister of Music and Church Organist of the Hartford Memorial Baptist Church in Detroit from 1983–1996. He was National Director of Music for the Progressive National Baptist Convention from 1990–1994 and National Music Director for the NAACP from 1988–1992.

Dr. Abbington is the author of *Let Mt. Zion Rejoice! Music in the African American Church* (Judson Press), *Readings in African American Church Music and Worship* (GIA Publications, Inc.), co-author of *Waiting to Go! African American Church Worship Resources from Advent through Pentecost* (GIA) and *Going to Wait! African American Church Worship Resources between Pentecost and Advent* (GIA); he edited Dr. Wyatt Tee Walker's *Spirits that Dwell in Deep Woods: The Prayer and Praise Hymns of the Black Religious Experience* (GIA) and is an associate editor of the best-selling *African American Heritage Hymnal* (GIA).

r i c h a r d   f l o y d

Richard Floyd is presently in his forty-second year of active involvement as a conductor, music educator, and administrator. He has enjoyed a distinguished and highly successful career at virtually every level of wind band performance, from beginning band programs through high school and university wind ensembles, as well as adult community bands. He serves as State Director of Music at the University of Texas at Austin, where he coordinates all facets of secondary school music competition for some thirty-five hundred performing organizations throughout the state. He is also musical director and conductor of the Austin Symphonic Band, which is viewed to be one of the premier adult concert bands in America.

Prior to his appointment at the University of Texas, Mr. Floyd served on the faculty at the University of South Florida as Professor of Conducting and at Baylor University in Texas, where he held the position of Director of Bands for nine years. His musical achievements include appearances at numerous state and regional music conferences, a distinguished performance for the 1977 College Band Directors National Association, the 1981 Music Educators National Conference, the 1989 Grand Finale Concert for the Midwest

International Band and Orchestra Clinic in Chicago, and the opening concert for the 1993 American Bandmasters Association Convention in New Orleans. The Austin Symphonic Band returned again in 1997 to the Midwest International Band and Orchestra Clinic to present the Grand Finale Concert. Performances by his various ensembles have been heard on radio broadcasts in both the United States and Europe. Before joining the faculty at Baylor, he taught junior high school and high school band in the Richardson, Texas public schools and served as music coordinator for that district's nationally acclaimed music program.

Mr. Floyd is a recognized authority on conducting, the art of wind band rehearsing, concert band repertoire, and music advocacy. As such, he has toured extensively throughout the United States, Canada, Australia, and Europe as a clinician, adjudicator, and conductor, including appearances in forty American states and in nine other countries. In 1997, he was a featured clinician for the Texas Music Educators Association, and in December of 1998, he presented a clinic, entitled "Rehearsal Magic," at the Midwest International Band and Orchestra Clinic.

Mr. Floyd has received the praise of numerous composers, including Ernst Krenek, Karel Husa, Roger Nixon, Frank Ticheli, Mark Camphouse, and Johan de Meij, for his insightful interpretation of their music. He is also co-author of *Best Music for Beginning Band,* published by Manhattan Beach Music. In 2002, he was the single recipient of the prestigious A.A. Harding Award presented by the American School Band Directors Association in recognition of his significant and lasting contributions to the school band movement.

During Mr. Floyd's professional career, he has held positions of leadership on many state and national committees for music education and wind music performance. He is a member of the American Bandmasters Association Board of Directors, John Philip Sousa Foundation Board of Directors, Chairman of the American

390 Bandmasters Association SpecialProjects/Commissioning Committee, an ex-officio member of the Texas Music Educator's Association Executive Board, and serves on the jury for the College Band Directors National Association Young Band Composition Competition. Since 1979, he has served as National Secretary of the College Band Directors National Association and has played an active leadership role in the implementation of this organization's many projects and services for twenty-five years.

allegra martin

Allegra Martin is a Master's degree student in conducting at Westminster Choir College, where she has studied with James Jordan, Andrew Megill, and Joseph Flummerfelt, among others. Growing up near Boston, she earned her undergraduate degree in physics and music at Williams College. Ms. Martin is the founder and director of Roseae Feminae, a women's chamber choir, and she is also the founder and previous director of New Century Voices, a new music chorus in Boston. She is also a singer, having most recently participated in the Spoleto Festival in Charleston, South Carolina, and the Lincoln Center Festival in New York. Active in tae kwon do, Ms. Martin earned her black belt in 2003 at the Jae H. Kim Tae Kwon Do Institute in Boston.

l. jackson newell

Jack Newell is University Professor Emeritus at the University of Utah (with which he has been associated since 1974) and currently Scholar-in-Residence at the Utah State Board of Regents. From 1995 to 2004, he served as president and senior professor at Deep Springs College in California. His scholarship and teaching encompass social ethics, the philosophy of leadership, and the history of universities.

From 1974 to 1990, Dr. Newell served as dean and principal

architect of the unique university-wide liberal arts and sciences

program at the University of Utah. This Liberal Education Program won national acclaim for its interdisciplinary undergraduate curriculum, strong faculty governance structure, imaginative teaching development incentives, and comprehensive course evaluation techniques. Under his leadership, the University launched two distinguished professorships—the McMurrin Professorship for visiting scholars and the University Professorship for University of Utah faculty.

While at Deep Springs College, Dr. Newell spearheaded a renaissance that renewed the college's educational vision, financial base, and physical plant. Founded in 1917, the college is an indirect legacy of American philosopher John Dewey. Its educational program is based on a demanding liberal arts curriculum, a student labor program anchored on sustainable agricultural and community practices, and student participation in every element of college governance. Located on a working ranch in a high desert valley east of the Sierra Nevada Range, this liberal arts college is one of the most innovative and competitive institutions of higher learning in the nation. Over the last six years, the students at Deep Springs have won one Rhodes Scholarship (2004) and six Harry S. Truman Scholarships, which are awarded nationally to the most promising public servants among American undergraduates.

Dr. Newell pursued his undergraduate degree at Deep Springs College and The Ohio State University, earned his M.A. in American and European history at Duke University, and his Ph.D. in the history and philosophy of European and American universities at Ohio State. He taught at Clemson University, Deep Springs College, and the University of New Hampshire before moving to the University of Utah. He has held visiting professorships in England, Canada, and New Zealand. He has also been called upon to advise academic leaders at over fifty universities throughout the United States and in Canada, China, Great Britain, Hungary, New Zealand, and The Bahamas.

392   Dr. Newell has published over one hundred articles and essays, and has written or edited nine books and monographs, including *Matters of Conscience: Conversations with Sterling McMurrin on Philosophy, Education, and Religion* (1996), a biographical study of the philosopher and social critic who served as United States Commissioner of Education during the administration of President John F. Kennedy. Among his other authored or edited works are *Creating Distinctiveness: Lessons from Uncommon Colleges and Universities* (1994), *A History of Thought and Practice in Educational Administration* (1987), and *The Students of Deep Springs College*, with Michael Smith and William Vollmann (2000). He has also served as editor of *The Review of Higher Education* from 1986 to 1991, and as co-editor of *Dialogue: A Journal of Mormon Thought* (an independent scholarly journal) from 1982 to 1987.

Dr. Newell was a founding trustee of the Bennion Center for Community Service at the University of Utah, and he has served in a variety of other voluntary organizations.

Among his honors, Dr. Newell has received the Joseph Katz Award for the Advancement of Liberal Learning (a national award, 1994) and appointment as the State of Utah's Carnegie-CASE Professor of the Year (1991). He is a former Presidential Teaching Scholar, and he also holds both the Hatch Prize for Teaching and the Distinguished Honors Professor Award at the University of Utah.

His persistent personal interests include writing, hiking, mountaineering, and landscape photography. He has traveled and photographed on the Antarctic Peninsula (2000), in the Alaskan bush (1997), in the Galapagos Islands (1990), and in China before modernization (1979).

kenneth r. raessler

Dr. Kenneth R. Raessler recently retired as Director of the School of Music at Texas Christian University (TCU). He was formerly

Director of Music in the Williamsport Area School District 393
(Williamsport, Pennsylvania). The Williamsport Music Education
Program achieved national prominence during his tenure, not only
for excellence in performance but also for excellence and innovation
in classroom music. The program was awarded the MENC Exemplary
Program Award in 1985.

Dr. Raessler holds a Bachelor's degree from West Chester
University in Pennsylvania, where he was named Distinguished
Alumni by both the University and the School of Music in 2003, a
Master of Music Education from Temple University, and a Ph.D. from
Michigan State University. He has taught in the public schools of East
Stroudsburg and Hatboro-Horsham, Pennsylvania, as well as
Belvidere, New Jersey. He also served for ten years as Director of
Music Education and Chairman of the Department of Music at
Gettysburg College.

A frequent guest speaker, lecturer, consultant, and clinician,
Dr. Raessler recently served as state president of the Texas Association
of Music Schools (TAMS) and College Chair and Vice President of the
Texas Music Educators Association from 1998–2000. He presented
invited papers at conferences of the National Association of Schools
of Music (NASM), and he served as a clinician at the 2004 Music
Educators National Conference and the 2003 Midwest International
Band and Orchestra Clinic as well as over twenty-five state music
conferences. He has presented keynote addresses for California Music
Educators Conference (CMEA); Florida Music Educators Conference
(FMEA); Nebraska Music Educators Conference (NMEA); New York
State School Music Association Summer Conference (NYSSMA);
South Carolina Music Educators Conference (SCMEA); Alberta,
Canada Music Educators Conference; Pennsylvania Music Educators
Conference (PMEA); and Georgia Music Educators Conference
(GMEA). He served as Consulting Editor of the Yamaha Corporation
publication *NEW WAYS* and has presented week-long summer
seminars on music administration at such schools as the Eastman

394

School of Music, The Hartt School of Music, Duquesne University, Villanova University, Texas Christian University, and VanderCook College. Dr. Raessler was interviewed in the March 1997 edition of *Instrumentalist* magazine, and he has served on the Board of Trustees of the Phi Mu Alpha Foundation. He has appeared in numerous *Who's Who* publications, including the 2003 and 2004 editions of *Who's Who in America,* and has received several Hall of Fame designations.

The author of over seventy articles, using his experiences as a catalyst, Dr. Raessler offers his recent book, *Aspiring to Excel,* as a challenge to all music educators to assess their priorities, their goals, and the sequence of instruction in their school district or their university. The book is designed to inspire leadership in the music educator through the investigation of many processes, and when these processes fall in place, students will then experience excellence through music, and music through excellence.

john yarrington

John Yarrington is Professor of Music, Director of Choral Studies, and Director of the School of Music at The Houston Baptist University. Nationally respected as a leader in church music, Dr. Yarrington is an accomplished conductor and composer. Additionally, he is director of the Chancel Choir at the First Presbyterian Church of Houston. He has served churches in Oklahoma, Arkansas, and Texas, and became renowned for the quality church music programs he built in those churches. He is in demand as both a guest conductor and clinician.

While in Texas, Dr. Yarrington founded the Arkansas Symphony Chorus, which he directed for five seasons, he was Interim Conductor of the Arkansas Symphony Orchestra for one season, and he served as Artistic Director of the Arkansas Chamber Singers. At Houston Baptist University, his choirs have distinguished themselves for their artistry and range of literature. In a recent residency, composer Morten Lauridsen said of the choir's work: "This was among the finest, both on a college and professional level. Their sense of pitch, vocal color, and interpretation of the music is very high."

Dr. Yarrington holds his Bachelor's and Doctor's degrees from The University of Oklahoma, as well as a Master of Sacred Music from Union Theological Seminary. An active contributor to professional journals, his writings on choral techniques, organization, and philosophy of church music are well known. His books include *Building the Youth Choir* (Augsburg Fortress), and his new book, *Somebody's Got My Hymnal* (Abington Press).

"Stupa and Flags"

Index of Quoted Persons